STARS, STRIPES AND CORPORATE LOGOS

DONALD L. GILLELAND

Black Rose Writing | Texas

ISBN: 978-1-68433-043-0
PUBLISHED BY BLACK ROSE WRITING
www.blackrosewriting.com

Printed in the United States of America
Suggested Retail Price (SRP) $18.95

Stars, Stripes and Corporate Logos is printed in Garamond Premier Pro

This book is dedicated to my wife, Peggy, with whom I have been in love my entire adult life. She inspires me, keeps me on a level plane, and makes me laugh like no one else can. She also edits everything I write.

Acknowledgement

A special acknowledgement to Marshall Frank, a well-respected and genuine Renaissance man: retired homicide detective, concert violinist, author of 14 books, mentor, and good friend, who encouraged me to write books as well as magazine and newspaper articles. Without Marshall's influence, this book would probably not have been written.

Another special acknowledgement to Francis J. Clifford, Esq., a friend, legal scholar, and generous soul who was gracious enough to lend his time and talents to edit this tome, and to create a name for it. I will forever be grateful Frank!

OTHER BOOKS BY DONALD L. GILLELAND

America: A Cultural Enigma

America: Where Great Things Happen

America: An Exceptional Nation

America: A Conflicted Nation

All are available on the Internet or from the publisher, Black Rose Writing, or directly from the author. Check out his webpage at www.donaldgilleland.com.

Things I Wish I'd Said

"America is another name for opportunity"
Ralph Waldo Emerson

"Everything has beauty, but not everyone sees it."
Confucius

"I will not let anyone walk through my mind with their dirty feet."
Mahatma Gandhi

"Illusions of grandeur are not the same as visions of greatness!"
Edwin Louis Cole

STARS, STRIPES AND CORPORATE LOGOS

PREFACE

There are all kinds of success and each can be defined differently. Too many people measure success by the almighty dollar. Wealthy people who make millions of dollars playing athletic games, recording music, or acting in a series of successful movies can be the envy of every young man or woman dreaming about their future.

In fact entertainers, which is what athletes, musicians, and actors are, tend to be the highest paid professionals in our society, more so than corporate chief executive officers, doctors, lawyers, college presidents, high school teachers, policemen, firemen, and military officers.

I'm not sure what that says about our society's system of values when we seem to appreciate somebody who can throw a football more than a researcher trying desperately to find a cure for Alzheimer's disease. It also strikes me as strange that the filthy rich don't always seem to be happy in their success.

The truth is that meaningful success can be measured in many ways that have little or nothing to do with how much an individual is paid or what his or her financial net worth is. While the rustle of new $20 bills can be a desirable sound of success for some people, the laughter of children playing in the backyard can be just as satisfying for a grandmother as she looks back over her life.

For many people money is irrelevant. Many very wealthy people were dead broke in their 20s. Some of them even spent time in jail or prison in their very young years, but turned their lives around at some point. It is not unusual for wealthy people to be envious of other less affluent people. While money may buy pleasantries, it doesn't always make its possessor happy.

The tabloids are full of titillating stories about supposedly successful people divorcing, marrying their fifth spouse, committing suicide or otherwise publicly displaying how truly unhappy they are despite their enormous wealth.

Success has a different meaning for each of us. The sound of success can be far less ostentations than driving around in a Lamborghini or a Maserati, both of which can cost more than twice what the average American makes in a year. The sound of success may be nothing more sensational than the sound of your future spouse approaching for your first date.

In 1936 Swami Sivanandaji Maharaj, founder of the Divine Life Society, defined success as always doing your best. "Put your heart, mind, intellect and soul into even your smallest acts. This is the secret of success," he said.

Celestine Chua, life coach, speaker, founder of Personal Excellence.com, says "success is believing you can." If you believe you can, you will succeed. "Success is 99% attitude and 1% aptitude," she claims. On the other hand, Dale Carnegie thinks believing is not enough. "You never achieve success unless you like what you are doing," he says.

Still, another definition of success is taking care of your own needs. Remember to put on your own oxygen mask before helping others. I'm confident airline executives would acknowledge the truth of this philosophy. Dodinsky, the one name author of the NY Times bestselling book *In the Garden of Thoughts,* says "be there for others, but never leave yourself behind."

Zig Ziglar, author of the book, *Secrets of Closing the Sale,* claims success is overcoming fear. And he too is right. Conquering fear makes one feel invincible. "Fear has two meanings: 'forget everything and run' or 'face everything and rise.' The choice is ours."

Michelangelo, the fifteenth century sculptor of *David* and the *Pieta,* believed success is learning something new each day. He understood that learning never stops. Perhaps one of his most famous quotes was "I am still learning," which he stated late in life.

Success can have a very personal sound to each of us. When asked about success Winston Churchill said: "Success is walking from failure to failure with no loss of enthusiasm." It can also be full of surprises. An old proverb reads, "Just when the caterpillar thought the world was ending, he turned into a butterfly."

Eleanor Roosevelt clearly had a much different vision of success. She once said: "Great minds discuss ideas; average minds discuss events; small minds discuss people."

For some people success may be the sound of a cash register ringing; for others it might be the sound of a boxer's glove as it strikes an opponent; or the sound of a cheering crowd as a marathoner crosses the finish line. The sound of success for a new mother might be the cry of a baby as it leaves the womb following a difficult birth.

I suspect everyone who reads this book will have a different way of looking at success. Over the years I had an unexpectedly satisfying and successful career that involved 30 years in the military and 10 years in the defense industry, followed by many years writing articles and books. For me, success had several different sounds.

At the end of this book, after I've discussed my life experiences and adventures, I will tell you what the sound of success is to me. Don't flip ahead and sneak a peek!

When I first looked back, my life seemed to be fairly simple, until I isolated separate chapters in an ongoing review of a continuous series of eventful episodes that no one in my family would ever have predicted.

I was raised in a very poor family. I and my siblings grew up in Alton, Illinois, a community of about 30,000 people situated on the Mississippi River, located about 15 miles northeast of St. Louis.

My family consisted of a dedicated, loving and hard working mother, a hopeless alcoholic house-painter father, and the wonder of three loving sisters and one brother, who is 15 years younger than me. He played no significant role in my upbringing.

Ours was a tight-knit, but struggling family, made more so by the nearly constant absence of an alcoholic father who wasted almost all of his weekly paychecks on booze. The consequences of his alcoholism will be evident as I describe Life in the Midwest in Chapter 1.

But it was and still is a loving family. I'm a hugger. Ours was a hugging family. With three sisters and a mother, all of whom required that I always hug them before leaving our house, I was so accustomed to hugging that I'm still a hugger today. As a church usher, I must hug 100 people a week. Hugging has become somewhat expected when I usher. In fact, some people who attend our church come down to the center aisle, where I usher, just to get a hug. They then return to their seats in the back of the church.

The rest of this book will be a discussion of evolving challenges played against a wonderful backdrop of exciting adventures that made up my life. I have visited 35 countries on five continents and found something to like about every one of them. Asia is wonderful, but so is Europe and Central America, although I was not fond of the continent of Africa. I was appalled by the extreme poverty I saw in Egypt.

While visiting Egypt in the mid-1980s, I stayed at the Heliopolis Hotel on the outskirts of Cairo. I understand that it has since burned down. It was a wonderfully elegant hotel that had a Mercedes Benz sitting in its parking lot in front of the hotel with gold trim everywhere one would normally expect to find chrome.

The division of mass classes was obvious everywhere I visited. Despite all the wealth I witnessed in the hotel, people were starving to death a few blocks down the street. There was a graveyard in the middle of the town, which I had to pass on my way to see the pyramids. What was appalling was the knowledge that entire families were living in the graveyard mausoleums.

Despite all the wonderful places I had visited, such as London, Paris, Stockholm, Israel, Caracas, Panama, Tokyo, Bangkok, Hong Kong, St Thomas, and Canadian cities such as Toronto, Montreal, Ottawa, Vancouver, and Windsor, after many years of travel, I concluded that I have never been anywhere in the world that I would rather live than right here in the United States. And by that, I mean *anywhere* in the United States.

When I served overseas in the military, my buddies and I often talked about "home." But home did not mean the state or city in which we were raised or from which we enlisted, it meant anywhere in the United States. As soon as we stepped down off an aircraft onto the tarmac anywhere in the United States, we were home.

Over the course of our marriage, my wife and I lived in 12 states, mostly on the northern tier where we were buried in snow every winter. Many of the states were quite lovely, but the weather was often brutal and I hated shoveling snow and ice.

My wife often said: "When you retire we're moving to a state where we never have to worry about snow again." I thought that was a marvelous idea. I looked forward to years of moderate, if not warm, weather.

Even though I loved the Midwest, I just couldn't stand the cold winters, and everything associated with it such as snow tires and heavy clothes. I didn't even like winter sports. Much of my life I was a long distance runner. I would run eight miles every day and sometimes 10-15 miles on the weekends. My wife also ran, although not quite as far as I ran. But when winter came, I almost always spent as much time as possible indoors, which included lots of time on racquetball courts because I didn't like to run outdoors in cold weather.

I became fairly proficient at racquetball, winning five trophies. Over the years I played moderately competitive racquetball about four times a week. But it was warmth not trophies that was my motivation for an indoor sport.

So, we spent all my vacation time during my last three professional years searching for the ideal retirement community. We started in the Carolinas, first North Carolina and then South Carolina. We also visited Georgia and finally Florida.

We visited each state during the summer and then during the winter. How else could we decide if snow was a possibility? As our search progressed we kept moving farther and farther south because even places we loved in the summer had winters we didn't like.

When we got to Florida, we first drove around the Panhandle, which is the arm of land extending from the far northeastern part of the Gulf of Mexico westward to Alabama and bordered by Georgia on the north. We liked the

Panhandle, but the winters get cold and occasionally get small amounts of snow. That wouldn't do!

We next drove down the east coast of Florida and liked the Melbourne area, about halfway down the state, but to do justice to the state, we thought it necessary to continue on south and to visit Fort Lauderdale and Miami and the west coast of Florida too.

We discovered the southern parts were too hot for us, especially the Miami and Naples areas, and the western part of the state seemed to be populated by an older generation of residents. As my wife observed, the western part of the state is populated by Q-tips: "skinny little necks with white tops," which is what we have become too!

As we left the western part of the state and crossed over once more to the eastern part, we remembered there was something we liked about the Melbourne area, so we revisited it. We fell in love with an unincorporated section just north of Melbourne named Suntree.

So, in 1993 we bought a half acre lot in an undeveloped subdivision named Summerwood, and built a 2,400 square foot house that quickly became our home, where we continue to live today 25 years later. Ours was the fourth house built in the Summerwood sub-division. That was quite an adjustment because in Michigan where we lived for the previous eight years, our house was a tad over 5,000 square feet, which we thought was way too much house for retirement.

To make the adjustment, we had to get rid of a lot of furniture. When I say a lot, I mean most of what we owned, because what looked good in Michigan didn't fit into the ambience of Florida. At least so said my wife! So we scaled down and bought a lot of new furniture. You will find more about life in Florida in Chapter 6.

For now, you need to know that the four most important influences in my life have not been anything associated with my time in the military or working in the corporate world. It has been two wonderful women, both of whom I have loved more dearly than anything else on God's green earth: my mother, Josephine, and my wife Peggy; and my Christian values and education, all of which made my lifetime challenges possible. But I'm getting ahead of myself.

Let's start my memoir.
Donald L. Gilleland

Chapter 1
Life in the Midwest

As mentioned in the Preface, I was born and spent all of my formative years in Alton, Illinois. It is just one of many small communities "across the river" from St. Louis.

I have survived cultural changes that were unimaginable then. There were no smartphones. We had a party line, with several neighbors sharing our telephone. Before we could place a call we had to listen to see if anyone else was using the line.

It was a time in which there were no air conditioners, ATMs, ballpoint pens, clothes dryers, contact lenses, copy machines (Xerox), credit cards, dishwashers, electric blankets, frozen foods, pantyhose, penicillin, polio shots, televisions, radar, fuel injected engines, or space exploration.

We dated, became engaged, got married, and had babies, in that order. Two people living together without the benefit of marriage was scandalous. We were one of the last generations to think that a woman should have a husband to have a baby, and that a father was an essential role model for the family. Having a meaningful relationship meant getting along well with your in-laws.

Divorce and pregnancy out of wedlock carried a severe stigma, as did filing for bankruptcy. There were no day care centers or nursing homes. Families took care of each other, and family doctors did everything else. Medical specialists were rare.

There were no electric typewriters, word processors, or computers, and hardware was something you got at the hardware store. Software was not even in the dictionary. Before refrigerators we had "ice boxes" that stored ice to keep our food fresh. Before oil and natural gas we heated our houses with coal, and had to "bank" the fire every night so it would still have embers in the morning.

There were no McDonalds or pizzas, but you could buy things in the five and ten store for 5 cents, get a two scoop ice cream cone for a nickel, and buy gasoline for 11 cents a gallon. There was no air conditioning. When it got hot we simply opened our windows and turned on fans.

*   *   *

"Made in Japan" meant junk and the United States was recognized as one of the world's leading manufacturers. We made most everything we used and grew most everything we ate.

Coke was a cold drink and pot was something you cooked in. If you couldn't get what you needed at the hardware store you probably had to order it from Sears & Roebuck or Montgomery Ward and wait several weeks for delivery.

There weren't any "no solicitation" signs in neighborhoods. Fuller Brush and Avon representatives knocked on doors regularly.

Weekend entertainment at the movies consisted of a Warner Pathe Newsreel, previews of coming attractions, a weekly serial, a cartoon and two feature length movies, all for less than 50 cents.

By today's standards we had a tough life, but we survived very nicely. We weren't as mobile a society as we are today. But, families were supportive, helped each other, and celebrated holidays together.

People born today will have more diverse problems and a much different look in their rearview mirror. Also, Midwesterners see life in the United States much differently than most American citizens see it. States that are part of the Midwest are generally considered to be Illinois, Indiana, Iowa, Kansas, Michigan, Minnesota, Missouri, Nebraska, North Dakota, Ohio, South Dakota, and Wisconsin.

According to the *Journal of Personality and Social Psychology*, "the old trope that Midwesterners are the friendliest people on earth might actually be rooted in truth." In my entire life I have never met anyone from the Midwest who is not friendly, even when they disagree with you politically. However, I still recommend not discussing politics and religion with people you don't know, unless you are comfortable with the prospects of rowdy and argumentative discussions. Being friendly doesn't mean being tolerant of opinions from loudmouths with whom you disagree.

As reported in "This is Why It's So Great To Be A Midwesterner, According to Science," by Sara Boboltz, *Huffington Post*, June 18, 2014, "We merely jumped at the chance to explain precisely what makes the midwestern region so wonderful, according to certain probably unbiased sources."

Here are their reasons: "It's been proven that Midwesterners are super friendly. They're eager to help out. International tourists find them charming. They have the most state pride. They're super interesting. Everything's so cheap! Midwestern air practically sparkles. Midwesterners' kindness extends even to their cars. They appreciate their teachers. They're a thrifty bunch of people. They're leading a pretty major linguistic change. Midwesterners value family, and keep them really close. "

In addition, researchers found that people who live in the more friendly and conventional Midwestern United States are also more likely to be conservative, less healthy, less educated, and less affluent. Researchers also noted that Midwesterners have more traditional values and that family and the status quo are extremely important.

The word Midwest has been in common use since the late 19th century. According to *Wikipedia*, the free encyclopedia, Midwesterners are sometimes viewed as open, friendly, and straightforward, or sometimes stereotyped as stubborn and uncultured.

It goes on to say Midwest values were shaped by religious beliefs and the agricultural values from the people who settled in the area. While other religions exist in the Midwest today, such as Catholicism, the Midwest is generally "a mix of Protestantism and Calvinism, untrusting of authority and power. "

Politics in the Midwest are divided, with many states leaning liberal and others conservative. The Great Lakes area, which has more large cities than the rest of the Midwest, tends to be the most liberal area of the Midwest, while the rural Great Plains states are more conservative.

Alton, Illinois, which is an amalgam of all of these values, was incorporated on October 10, 1877. Its elevation is 520 feet, its land area encompasses 15.6 square miles, and its population density is 1,737 people per square mile.

According to Alton's web page its ancestral make-up in 2013 was primarily German, followed by Irish, English, and pure United States, with some Italian and French. Incidentally, my wife and I are both mostly Irish, although I am also British, Cherokee, Dutch, and French, with an Irish name. Incidentally we visited Ireland for 10 days in 2012 and discovered there is an entire clan of Gillelands there, but there are also some in Scotland.

Alton has remained fairly static over the years. When I was born in 1935, the population was about 30,000. According to Alton's official web page its population in 2014 was 27,177. As cities go, it's an average and fairly representative example of the Midwest.

Further evidence of Midwestern values in Alton was the annual 4th of July celebration. As a child growing up in Alton, I cherished that celebration. Alton residents lined up on Broadway, the main thoroughfare, at what then seemed like a huge parade came through town. The parade included marching bands and all kinds of patriotic participants that enchanted young boys and girls. It was always an exciting time to be living in Alton, and we eagerly anticipated that parade.

The only rival to that annual parade was the occasional carnival or the Ringling Bros or Barnum & Bailey Bros. circus that came to town. It didn't matter to us which it was; both were always exciting to see. We loved watching elephants and horses and other animals parade through downtown on the way to their ultimate destination. It was especially exciting for members of my family because we couldn't afford the entrance price to actually see the carnival or circus performances. Occasionally we were able to sneak into the circus grounds to look around but we couldn't afford to buy a ticket to any of the shows or exhibits. It was just grand to look around at all the seemingly wondrous stuff.

In 1954, a year after I graduated from high school, the city of Alton was named as one of the three finalists for the location of the new United States Air Force Academy. Eventually, Alton lost to the winning site of Colorado Springs, Colorado, but Alton residents still remember all the excitement generated by the prospect of having the new Air Force Academy located there. Nobody did anything foolish like investing in prospective land sites or anything like that. Everyone dreamed of the potential boost it would likely have been to Alton's economy.

Alton was also known for being the site of the last Abraham Lincoln and Stephen Douglas debate in October 1858, and the location of a state penitentiary that was used during the Civil War to hold up to 12,000 Confederate prisoners of war.

Other notable celebrities for which Alton has been known over the years include: Miles Davis, jazz musician; Ezekiel Elliott, running back for the Dallas Cowboys; Mary Beth Hughes, movie actress; Elijah Lovejoy, abolitionist; John M. Olin, inventor, industrialist and philanthropist; Edward O'Hare, Medal of Honor recipient; William S. Paley, founder and CEO of CBS Corporation; James Earl Ray, assassin of Martin Luther King, Jr.; Phyllis Schlafly, conservative author, constitutional lawyer and activist; Paul Tibbets Jr, pilot of the Enola Gay, which dropped the Atom Bomb on Hiroshima, Japan; Lyman Trumbull, U.S. Senator from Illinois and coauthor of the 13th Amendment to the U.S. Constitution; and Rick Yager, cartoonist.

During the 1980s and 1990s many of Alton's manufacturing facilities closed and with their closing Alton lost a lot of jobs as it shifted from being a manufacturing center to becoming a tourist attraction with its Mississippi River floating casino.

During my formative years, Alton was an interesting little city, and I didn't venture outside its city limits by more than 50 miles until after my high school graduation. But I did own a car I loved. My Grandfather, who was actually my step-grandfather because my Grandma had divorced my grandfather and remarried, helped me finance my first car by extending a loan to me with scheduled payments to him until I paid it off.

It was a wonderful learning experience for a 16-year old boy. My step-grandfather knew that I was industrious and always had a job, so unless something dramatic happened to me, he could depend on me to repay the loan. He kept a record of the loan and payments in a log book in his Justice of the Peace office. I made weekly payments to him until I repaid his loan. I loved that he was willing to help me buy my first car. Actually I loved him and my Grandma a lot. They were both especially kind to our family and often had us kids over to spend the nights with them. But I always remembered how gracious he was in helping me buy my first car.

I first bought a 1940 Plymouth that didn't last long. While waiting in a left turn lane on Broadway, our major thoroughfare, I was hit from behind by another car, and it totaled my car. I next bought a 1938 Ford that my friends and I fell in love with. It served me well throughout high school until my graduation when I joined the U.S. Navy. I'll cover more on that in Chapter 2.

To put southern Illinois into a regional perspective, keep in mind that Illinois is 373 miles long and borders on Kentucky. It has been my experience that when people think of Illinois, they generally think of Chicago and have little or no idea that Illinois borders on Kentucky to the south. They rarely think of Carbondale, which is where Southern Illinois University is located or Cairo, which is at the southern tip of Illinois, as areas significantly different than the greater Chicago area. In truth, the southern tip of Illinois had more in common with Kentucky than with northern Illinois.

Over the years I've discovered that a lot of people don't known that southern Illinois has very little in common with northern Illinois. Even today, southern Illinois is agrarian and is made up of farmland and coal mines. You can drive for miles without seeing anything but farmland and cows. On the other hand, northern Illinois is industrial. It's made up of factories and larger cities such as Chicago.

What this means is that people who think of Chicago have no real feel for what life is like in southern Illinois. Chicago has a faster pace, while southern Illinois is more laidback and casual.

Deadbeat Dad

My father was a brute of an alcoholic who spent most, if not all, of his paychecks on booze. By brute I don't mean he was big. He was barely 5' 8" tall and weighed about 160 lbs. until late in life when he climbed to over 200 pounds.

But he was mean-spirited and when he drank alcohol, especially beer, he thought he was tough. He was a beer alcoholic and would start fights in Alton's bars and take on all comers. He rarely won, but that didn't keep him from believing he could. The consequence was that he spent a lot of nights in the local jail. His stepfather bailed him out of jail more times than any of us could remember. His mother, our grandma, always made excuses for him, even knowing of his problems. She would send her husband, our step-grandpa, down to the local jail to bail him out, but our dad never seemed to be embarrassed by his constant problems.

He had a caring brother with whom he had nothing in common. His brother was a sober, reliable, family oriented Christian who carried mail for the U.S. Postal Service. He also had a wonderful sister who made a living throughout her life as a hairdresser. Both his brother and his sister were especially loving toward our family, as was his mother and stepfather. I frequently stayed at the home of my Grandma and Grandpa, as they were affectionately known, throughout the year. I loved visiting with them because they seemed wealthy contrasted with our family, and they lived on one of Alton's main streets with wonderful views of a constant stream of traffic. For as long as I could remember, Grandpa would use me as an underage witness whenever he married someone in a civil ceremony in his office.

He would give me about 50 cents as an unofficial payment for being a witness.

Whenever I visited with them Grandma would immediately send Grandpa to the grocer store to buy a pound of hamburger and buns that she always prepared for my lunch. I can't explain why, but her hamburgers always tasted better than hamburgers I ate anywhere else. To this day I still salivate whenever I think about those hamburgers. Some 60 years later I still have never found anyone else, private or commercial, who can make hamburgers taste as good as those made by Grandma. I always wondered why my Grandma and Grandpa couldn't do anything to control my father.

The problem was that my father continually embarrassed his siblings and his parents, as well as his own family. As if that wasn't bad enough, my grandparents on my mother's side of the family constantly distanced themselves from us because they believed, rightfully so, that my father was a deadbeat. I had trouble understanding why they treated the rest of us badly because of their disrespect for my father. Even as a child it never seemed fair, either to us or to my mother. But it never changed over the years. Most of the aunts, uncles, and cousins on that side of the family died without ever embracing anyone in our family. They just could never get over the fact that according to them, my mother married down from them on their social ladder. Why they felt as they did about us kids I never understood.

On the other hand, besides making his living as a union house painter, my father was an extraordinarily gifted artist who painted landscapes and other scenic pictures that showcased a spectacular talent. He painted in oils and while painting he was so single-focused I could walk up and stand right next to him and he wouldn't even know I was there.

His paintings didn't sell for much, but always seemed to be in demand. Some of them still hang in regional galleries in and around Alton. He also painted detailed landscapes on the sides of buildings. At another time in history he might have become a great artist, but it just wasn't to be! Booze got in the way of his talent.

Before the start of World War II, while my father was in his 30s, he was funny and animated. He constantly did funny things to amuse me and my siblings, as well as other kids in our neighborhood. In some ways the kids viewed him as a neighborhood clown. He constantly entertained us and all the kids loved him.

For instance, he would carve apples or various pieces of fruit to form protrusions out of his mouth to make funny faces to amuse or scare the kids. He had other talents too, which I'll get to in a moment.

Our neighborhood was fairly small. Our street was barely a half-mile long and ended at what was then a 27-acre farm that grew tomatoes, asparagus, and various berries. Eventually the farmer's house burned down from a cause I never knew and he sub-divided his 27-acres into lots that he sold to housing developers. Today the street on which I was raised is longer with all 27-acres of that farmland built out with homes.

We lived in a very modest one-bedroom house on the outskirts of town. Of course a one-bedroom house didn't accommodate a family of six very well. For a while we put a couple of single beds in the dining room and another couple in the living room, but that didn't work very well either. So my dad and his stepfather, both of whom were very handy with tools, cut a hole in the dining room ceiling and put in a stairway to the attic. Then they put in studs, wallboard, and flooring and created three bedrooms in the attic. They were not really rooms in the traditional sense; they were just small spaces into which we were able to place our beds.

The rooms weren't tall enough to stand in so we had to walk bent over, and other than the stairway there were no wall partitions between the rooms, but it was wonderful to have our own bedrooms. I'm sure it wouldn't seem like much to affluent families, but for us it was a grand step up from sleeping in the living and dining rooms. We thought it was wonderful!

In 1941, after the Japanese bombed Pearl Harbor, the United States entered the war. Of course my father and uncles, except for one uncle, all joined the navy and we didn't see them again for a bit over three years. All of them served on ships in the Pacific. The one exception was an uncle on my mother's side who served in the army in Europe.

My father's personal problems began while he was in the U.S. Navy during 1942-1945. He served as a seaman aboard the *USS Natoma Bay (CVE-62)*, a small escort aircraft carrier that none of us had ever heard of.

At 06:35, June 7, 1945, after having maneuvered through typhoon weather, the *USS Natoma Bay* was attacked by a suicidal Japanese "Zero" aircraft, broad on the port quarter and low on the water. Changing course, the enemy aircraft came in over the stern, fired incendiary ammunition at the bridge, and on reaching the island structure, nosed over and crashed on the flight deck. The engine, propeller, and a bomb tore a hole in the flight deck, 12 feet by 20 feet, while the explosion of a bomb it was carrying damaged the deck of the foc'sle and the anchor windlass beyond repair and ignited a nearby American navy fighter aircraft.

My father wasn't hurt by the "Zero" attack, and he served on the aircraft carrier in the Pacific until he was discharged in 1945, at which time he brought home with him a piece of the Japanese "Zero" that had crashed on his ship. I have no idea how he got to keep the souvenir piece; he never told us how he did it. He also brought home with him a Japanese sword, but he never explained how or why he got that either.

He never explained to any of us why he felt compelled to carry a piece of that "Zero" and the sword home with him from the Pacific; but, over the years, both disappeared and to this day I don't know what ever became of them.

According to the Department of Defense's Manual of Military Decorations and Awards, Volume 3, the *USS Natoma Bay* earned seven battle stars for her World War II service on the Asiatic-Pacific theater medal and two bronze stars on the Philippine Liberation medal. The *USS Natoma Bay* also earned a Presidential Unit Citation, taking part in 13 major operations in World War II.

Even though the damages to the ship had been repaired, on July 30, 1959, the *USS Natoma Bay* was decommissioned and sold as scrap to Japan, which somehow didn't seem fitting since their aircraft nearly destroyed it at sea.

My father never spoke much about his naval experiences; he never told us how much the "Zero" attack or any other combat experience affected him, but it was after he came home that he began to drink copious amounts of beer, staying away from his family for long periods.

He would come home drunk, collapsing on our living room floor where he would lay until he slept off his stupor enough to nurse his hangover. He would never explain to any of us why he drank so much or how he came to be drunk every week, especially after payday.

One of my earliest Christmas memories was watching two of his friends from work carry my passed-out drunken father into our house and drop him on the living room floor where he spent the day in a stupor while we celebrated Christmas without him.

He was the worst possible example of a father for a young boy. I can still vividly remember one night when he came home drunk and entered our house through the basement and climbed up the stairway leading to our kitchen, all the while yelling profanities at my mother. As he approached the doorway into the kitchen, at the top of the steps, my mother hit him over the head with a rolling pin and knocked him back down the stairs. He laid on the basement floor all night until he slept off his drunken condition. The next morning he couldn't remember how he got home, why he was in the basement, or why his head hurt so much. None of us said anything to him about it.

Over the next several years we witnessed many other similar experiences until he eventually abandoned our family completely while my mother was eight months pregnant with her fifth child. She had mistakenly thought if she allowed herself to get pregnant again it would keep him home, but that was not the case. Even with his drunken history she literally begged him to stay, but he deserted us anyway.

In 1951 my father moved to Tucson, Arizona, where he met and married another woman. He returned to Alton only once to attend the funeral of one of my sisters, and that was the only time any of us ever saw him after he abandoned the family. Ironically he begged me to give him money for a bus ticket to get back to Tucson, which I did—never expecting to get it back. And, of course, I didn't.

He died in Tucson at the age of 75, and no one from our family attended his funeral; however, his mother and stepfather understood that we were not the cause of his personality defects and they continued to treat us with love and kindness throughout their lives.

Once he abandoned our family he refused to pay child support to my mother, but for a reason she never explained, she would not seek his arrest or prosecution. She worked two jobs to support us. From the time my father abandoned our family, my mother didn't want to hear any of us mention him. He was simply a forbidden topic in our family household.

Religious Lessons

While my father did not ever seem to have a religious belief of any kind, my mother was a devout Roman Catholic who put great faith in Jesus. She attended church as regularly as she could and prayed daily, sometimes often throughout the day, and always had a list of people for whom she prayed.

For mom, everything in her life was judged based on how she thought it pleased or displeased Jesus. All of us kids frequently disappointed mom if we didn't live up to her Christian standards, but she was rarely judgmental about her disappointment with us. She believed common sense was a good yardstick, but her Christian sense was by far the better measuring tool. The lesson she taught each of us was that we should measure life by how we thought our conduct pleased or disappointed Jesus.

Mom never referred to Jesus as Jesus Christ. He was just Jesus. Today many, if not most, Christians refer to Jesus Christ as though Jesus is His first name and Christ is His last name. Of course in the first century there were no last names. Jesus was His name and Christ simply meant Messiah. So Jesus Christ literally means Jesus the Messiah, but somehow that gets lost in the translation today as Christians continue to refer to Him as Jesus Christ.

It was my mother who first shared with us the fact that we didn't own anything. Everything we had belonged to God, and we were merely temporary custodians of it. At the end of our brief temporal existence on Earth we would not be able to take anything with us to heaven, and God would judge us based on how well we used our time and talents on earth. Of course it was many years before the truth of her wisdom caught hold of me.

While most of my life I thought of myself as a Christian, because of my Roman Catholic experiences, it was not until I visited Israel in 2004 that I fully committed myself to Jesus and his teachings. I can still remember when it occurred. It was in mid-November, while we were on a boat in the middle of the Sea of Galilee, that I felt the physical presence of God. It was transformational. I had never experienced anything like that earlier in my life.

Nevertheless, my mother was a near perfect Christian example. She raised all of us to be Roman Catholics, although none of us shared her deep faith in Catholicism. While we all went to a Catholic elementary school and later attended Catholic catechism classes while attending public schools, we always felt there was something missing. Later as adults we each gravitated toward Protestantism, although for several years as a preteen I served as an altar boy at our local Roman Catholic Church.

In those days the Catholic Mass was said in Latin, and I had to memorize a lot of the ritual so I could respond to the prayers being said by the priest. I can't explain it, but even to this day I can still recite the opening Latin phrases with which I responded to the Roman Catholic priest:

The priest would open the Mass with: "In nomine Patris, et Filii, et Spiritus Sancti. Amen." He would then say "Introibo ad altare Dei," which meant "I enter the alter of God."

I would respond "Ad Deum qui laetificat juventutem meam," which meant" Unto God who gives joy to my youth."

I served as an altar boy for quite a few years as a preteen, feeling important all the while because of what I perceived as a significant function that would bring me closer to Jesus.

I have no idea why I still remember those words. Perhaps it was because my mother was always so immensely proud of the fact that I had been an altar boy.

My siblings and I attended St. Mary's Catholic school for our early elementary education. However, one day after riding home from school on a pubic bus my oldest sister stepped behind the bus to cross the street without watching. She walked right into the path of a car. She was hit by the car and suffered moderate injuries. After that my mother was afraid for us to ride the public bus to the Catholic school in the center of town, so she withdrew us from St. Mary's and enrolled us in a local public school located at the end of the street on which we lived.

I could never fathom the rationale for her decision since to get to the public school we still had to cross the same street on which my sister was hit by a car. Nevertheless, we all finished our education in public schools.Despite the evolving secularization of America, Alton is still mostly a Christian city. During the 1940s there was no such thing as "separation of church and state." It was not uncommon to see bibles and hear religious instruction in public places. Public prayers said at graduations, public meetings and public sporting events were common. Even state and federal legislatures opened with prayers and the mention of Jesus was routinely overheard in opening prayers in Congress.

None of this was uncommon. It seemed to be part of the Midwestern culture that everyone we knew took for granted. Prayer was simply the beginning and ending of nearly every public event I ever attended in Alton, and I don't remember ever hearing anyone from Alton objecting to it.

Even today, according to CNN, over 75 percent of Americans call themselves Christian. Even though that figure is less than it was 20 years ago when it was 85 percent, we are still the largest Christian population in the world, even larger than

Brazil, which until recently had the largest Roman Catholic population in the world.

Even amidst a growing secularization of the United States, historians still point out that our nation was founded on Judeo/Christian principles because the Founding Fathers recognized the value of these principles in creating a moral and virtuous society. For the first 200 years of our existence, we were universally recognized as a nation founded on Judeo/Christian principles, with freedom to practice our religious beliefs unfettered by any kind of government intrusion or restrictions. God is even mentioned four times in our Declaration of Independence, one of our most precious and revered documents.

In 1864 we added "In God We Trust" to a newly designed coin. In 1954, President Eisenhower approved the addition of "under God" to our Pledge of Allegiance. "So help Me God" was also added as a suffix to the oaths of office for federal judges. In 1956 we adopted "In God We Trust" as our national motto, and "In God We Trust" was added to our paper currency in 1957.

Interestingly enough, all 50 states acknowledge God in their state constitutions. The president of the United States places his hand on a Bible while being sworn into office. The United States Senate and the United States House of Representatives each has an official government chaplain and they begin each day with a prayer.

Many of our federal buildings in the nation's capitol, Washington, DC, including the U.S. Supreme Court, have engravings that recognize God as our creator.

The front of the U.S. Supreme Court building has an engraving of Moses holding the Ten Commandments. The courts have pretty much decided those ten commandments cannot be put on public display in a government building, but they are still engraved on the entrance to the highest court in our land.

We have allowed atheists and agnostics to secularize much of our society, but while they haven't succeeded completely, they have made huge strides toward removing God and prayer from the public square, even though Christmas is still a national holiday.

It is ironic that we can celebrate the birth of Jesus the Christ as a nation, but we can't display a crèche, representing His birth, on public property, and we cannot offer prayers anywhere on pubic property.

It is also ironic that it is perfectly proper for the government to give employees a paid holiday to celebrate the day on which we commemorate the birth of Christ, and pay them to take the day off to celebrate this Christian holiday—as long as they don't do so on public property.

However, I also note that atheists and agnostics never ever insist on going to work during the Christmas holiday, and I note that we have been a Christian nation continuously since 1776. It is even more important to remember that Jesus may soon return and there can be no compromise with the reality of that truth.

I have never had any trouble defending the concept of the Christian salvation message, which is simply this: if you believe that Jesus is the divine Son of God, who sacrificed His life on the cross for our sins, was resurrected from the dead to prove there is life after death, and invite Him into your life as the ultimate model, you will be saved.

The reason I have no problem with defending this message without religion or the Bible is because all of it can be verified independently without any religious reference. The Romans publicly verified that they killed Him, and once He was resurrected from the dead more than 500 people witnessed His presence over the next 30 days. That is all historical fact that can be verified without a single religious reference. Skeptics need only do some serious reference searches without relying on the holy Bible.

Pray that He continues to bless our country and that we will soon return to the biblical standards of the Ten Commandments that are carved into the U.S. Supreme Court building.

In December 2003 my mother died at the age of 92, before there was a pronounced effort to eradicate religion and prayers from public life. While it is true that Madalyn Murray O'Hair led an effort to ban public prayer in 1962, the movement didn't really pick up until much later. It is also interesting to note that O'Hair's son has become a Christian.

My mom prayed the rosary every day and worshiped Jesus as her Savior. She completely believed the way to heaven was to acknowledge the Christian salvation message. She was absolutely certain that anyone who does that would spend eternity in heaven with God. For those who are interested, my wife and I share my mom's religious belief in the salvation message. She would not be happy that we are no longer Roman Catholic, but she would be pleased that we know, accept, and trust in the salvation message.

She would turn over in her grave if she knew that public prayers have become so homogenized they are no longer recognizable as being distinctly Christian, and that the First Amendment to the U.S. Constitution guaranteeing "freedom of religion" is no longer sacrosanct.

She would have been horrified to read that a Christian baker could be forced by our justice system to bake a wedding cake for a same-sex couple or be forced out of business, or that failure of a justice of the peace to marry same-sex couples could cost him his justice of the peace position, even though his Christian belief system does not acknowledge same-sex unions.

Even 65 years ago as a devout Roman Catholic my mother did not believe in divorce. She believed marriage was blessed by God and was a one-time event between a man and a woman and was supposed to last until the death of one of the spouses. She held tightly to those beliefs, but in time she divorced my father not because she changed her beliefs, but because he did not share her beliefs and begged her to divorce him. She eventually granted his wish and divorced him. But, for the rest of her life, my mother considered herself to be a married woman and honored her marital commitment, refusing to even consider dating another man. She died at age 92 without ever dating anyone after my father abandoned her.

Mother's Influence

As I was growing up my mother became my hero. Every positive value I have I got from her. While she was basically unskilled in the traditional sense, while my father was away at war, she took in washing and ironing to make ends meet. Think about that for a moment. She washed and ironed other peoples' clothes, slaving over a washing machine in our basement every day, after which she stood over a hot ironing board for hours just to earn modest amounts of money to help her raise us kids.

I still have a scar on the base of the little finger on my right hand from sticking my hand in the washing machine ringer while my mom was holding me in her arms. The ringer ran my arm all the way up past my elbow, but instead of hitting the emergency release my mother put the ringer in reverse and ran my arm back out again. I almost lost my little finger. Of course I don't remember any of this because I was so young when it happened, but I have a long scar at the base of my finger as evidence of it.

I didn't realize how poor we were until neighbors began bringing us bags of groceries because they knew my mother was struggling to feed us. It was embarrassing to acknowledge to other kids that we were so poor we had to accept charity. Until then I had never really thought too much about the fact we didn't ever seem to have as much money as other families. I thought everyone was probably having the same kind of problems we were having. I thought it was normal to eat peanut butter and jelly sandwiches and cereals as primary sources of food. Even today, I still love peanut butter and jelly sandwiches. Before we had peanut butter and jelly we often ate lard and tomato sandwiches.

After my father abandoned us, mom worked as a clerk at the Famous and Barr Company, a division of Macy's department store headquartered in St. Louis. She walked a half-mile from our house to get to a bus stop. Then she took the city bus to downtown Alton and connected to another bus to take her to St. Louis. It was a very long commute to her work place and a very long commute to get back home at the end of the day. But mom didn't seem to mind. I cannot remember ever hearing her complain about her lot in life. She just did what was necessary to keep the family going.

Mom worked at the Famous and Barr Company for several years until she got a job as a telephone operator at the Illinois Bell Telephone Company in Alton, where she retired after 20 years. Mom always spoke in glowing terms about her job at the telephone company. As far as she was concerned the Alton Illinois Bell Telephone Company helped her to save the life of our family, for which she was always thankful.

I was fifteen when my father abandoned us. My three sisters were a few years younger than me and my new brother was 15 years younger. My mom made it clear to me that she did all she could do to support my four siblings. She expected me to help by sharing with my siblings whatever modest amounts of money I earned.

An Early Work Ethic

I didn't mind helping because whatever cultural and religious values I had were gleaned from examples my mother set for us. Besides, unlike young millennials today, many of whom are supported by their parents from birth through college and sometimes later, I started working at age 12. By working, I don't mean I was gainfully employed at that young age, but I did whatever I could to earn money.

We had a wonderful wooded area across the street from our house, an area that extended for more than 27 acres running all the way to railroad tracks on which the cargo and passenger trains passed through Alton on the way to and from Chicago. As a pre-teen I would dig up sassafras roots, cut them, clean them, and put them into bunches that I could sell door to door. Neighbors couldn't believe I was doing it, but people bought them from me to make sassafras tea. Today there are so many commercial brands available, I doubt anyone ever thinks about making sassafras tea.

Another adventure I had as a young teenager was making clothes props. In those days after washing their clothes nearly everyone hung their clothes on clotheslines in their back yards to dry. In the 1940s we didn't have clothes dryers. I would cut down saplings having a proper "Y" joint, cut them off at an appropriate length, trim them, skin them, and sell them door-to-door to be used as clothes props to hold up the clothes lines.

Because the weight of wet clothes would cause the clothes lines to sag, clothes props were needed to hold up the line so the clothes wouldn't drag on the ground. Everybody needed clothes props and business was good until I ran out of saplings to cut down. The owners of the property weren't too happy about me cutting down their saplings, so even if business wasn't good I soon had to do something else.

So I continued to find ways to make money. In the winter I shoveled snow; in the summer I cut grass. When I turned 14, I got a newspaper route delivering the *St. Louis Globe-Democrat*, a morning newspaper for the greater St. Louis area, and the *Alton Evening Telegraph*, a local Alton newspaper, to neighbors living on two adjacent streets. I got up early in the morning and delivered the *Globe-Democrat* so people could read it before they went to work. In the evening I delivered the *Telegraph*.

Some of my friends who also delivered newspapers had trouble collecting the cost every week for the papers they delivered. I developed a technique that ensured my collection payments would be made promptly. I collected for my weekly deliveries every Saturday. After a few people made it a habit of not being home when I collected on Saturday, I made it clear to everyone that those who would not be home on Saturday should leave the payment on their front porch where I could pick it up when I made my rounds on Saturday.

The catch was that I also made it clear those who did not pay on Saturday would be awakened by a knock on their front door early Sunday morning for collection. If they missed two weeks of payment by not being home on two consecutive weekends, I would stop delivery of their newspaper until they resumed payment. A few people complained to the newspaper office but the newspaper executives supported my approach. After two months of this experience, I never had any more trouble with collections. Everybody paid one way or another on Saturday.

It was as a paperboy that I developed what would become a lifetime preference for ice cream. There was a "mom and pop shop," a small grocery store on my paper route that also sold ice cream cones. I learned my first barter lesson at an early age on that paper route. Every day I gave them a free evening newspaper and they gave me a free two-scoop ice cream cone.

I must point out a significant difference between then and now. In 1940 I could get a two-scoop ice cream cone for a nickel. Unfortunately today that same ice cream cone costs at least $5.00, sometimes more if the two scoops are put on a waffle cone.

To be fair, I should also point out that a nickel newspaper now costs about a dollar. But, as you can see, the 67-year difference for the ice cream cone is far greater than the 67-year difference for the newspaper. There are other significant differences too. While I was a 14-year-old paperboy, I was quite satisfied with a two-scoop ice cream cone. Today, a two-scoop ice cream cone only makes me want a pint. Also, as a 14-year-old I doubt I weighed more than 135 pounds. Today I weigh 220 pounds, part of which is the result of my long-time consumption of ice cream and other sugary carbohydrates. As an aside, I am a sugar-addicted diabetic, which is somewhat of an oxymoron that I have to deal with, which means I have to keep track of my glucose readings and insulin injections.

Nevertheless, to this day I cannot pass by an ice cream shop. It is my all time favorite treat, especially raspberry-ripple ice cream. Some places that carry it even include small pieces of chocolate embedded in the ice cream. I prefer it without the chocolate, but I'll take raspberry-ripple almost any way I can get it. Lordy, Lordy, just thinking about that makes me want to abandon this computer and go get some!

For a short period in the late 1940s I delivered Grit, formerly a weekly newspaper, now an all-glossy, perfect bound bimonthly magazine format. It was popular in the rural United States during much of the 20th century. It carried the subtitle "America's Greatest Family Newspaper." In the early 1930s it targeted small town and rural families with 14 pages plus a fiction supplement. By 1932 it had a circulation of 425,000 in 48 states, and 83% of its circulation was in towns having a population of fewer than 10,000 people. During the 1940s mostly children and teenagers sold it.

When I turned 16, I abandoned the newspaper business and started working in local movie theaters. During the 1940s and 1950s, Alton had five indoor movie theaters and one outdoor drive-in movie theater. From time to time I worked in two of the indoor theaters and the drive-in theater as an usher/parking attendant.

Movie theaters were much different in the 1940s and 1950s. Ushers made sure nobody snuck into the theater through the exit doors. Sometimes young kids would pool their money to buy one ticket and then the ticket holder would open an exit door to let in his friends so they could see the movie without buying a ticket. It was part of my job to see that didn't happen.

At the drive-in movie it was not uncommon for teenagers to pile into the trunk of a car and wait for the driver and one passenger to buy a ticket and drive into the theater before they abandoned the trunk and got into the back seat. I patrolled the parking area and sometimes caught them doing this. After I would report them to the office, the kids and their car would be escorted off of the property. Sometimes I would catch kids sneaking into the movie property from the wooded area in the back of the theater lot, where they would stand around listening to the movie on a car speaker. When I caught them they too were escorted off the property.

Ushers were also expected to keep the audience quiet so patrons didn't disturb others sitting around them. Today there are no movie theater ushers, and rude people unconsciously disturb their neighbors by holding discussions out loud as though they were sitting in their living room. My wife and I haven't attended an evening movie for many years because of that. I used to confront talkers by asking them to keep their voices down to a whisper. My wife hated it when I did that.

I remember one time when a couple two rows behind us at a movie theater were discussing the movie so loud that it was very disruptive. I turned around and not too gently asked them to keep their voices down to a whisper. The lady turned to her boyfriend/husband and said to him "leave the little guy alone; he could be dangerous." I didn't notice until after I confronted them that he was about 6' 5" contrasted to my 5' 8." But the important thing was that they shut up for the rest of the movie.

Now we go to early afternoon movies, which are rarely crowded. Even so, I still have to occasionally confront people who use their smartphones during the movie. Actually in a darkened theater the light from a smartphone is more distracting than the sound is.

Life is different in Alton today. When I visited there recently I noticed that there are no movie theaters of any kind. All five of the indoor theaters and the drive-in movie theater closed with the advent of the Internet, closed circuit television, Netflex, VHS, and DVDs. Now anyone who wants to see a movie in a theater must travel to a neighboring community, watch movies streaming on TV or buy DVDs when they become available and watch the movies at home. That was a huge surprise for me because I had spent so much of my time as a teenager working in the movie theaters. I noticed that the few theater buildings still standing are repurposed. I have no idea what they are used for today, but seeing them was a nostalgic experience for me.

Wanting to make more money at age 16, I began working behind the counter at a fast food restaurant, where I did a little bit of everything from waiting on customers to wiping the counters, sweeping the floors, and washing the windows. That was one of my less enjoyable jobs as a young man, and I didn't last long there. Don't get me wrong; I didn't get fired. I just hated the work and immediately started looking for some other way to earn money.

Once I got my driver's license at age 16, I applied to and was hired by a local florist to drive a panel truck delivering flowers. While it was a lot better than working in a fast food restaurant, it was only a stopgap until I could find something that offered a better work outlook and more pay while I was in high school.

That opportunity came while I was a junior in high school. I found a job as a pinsetter in a local bowling alley. The pay was better than delivering flowers, and coincidentally I found I had some skill as a bowler. The owner would let us pinsetters bowl for free as long as we left the lights off and bowled in the dark. Even as a young boy I was proficient enough to carry a 170 average, so occasionally when a bowling team was short a player the owner would stick me in as a substitute bowler. The only problem with that I was not getting paid for the evening, but I did earn some favors with the owner for serving as a substitute on one of his favorite teams.

There was also a pool table in the center of the eating area of the bowling alley, and the proprietor would allow us pinsetters to shoot pool for free when the table was not in use as long as we left the table light off. I would play pool during our down time when no one was bowling and a pinsetter wasn't needed. Consequently I became a pretty good pool player, not quite a shark but good enough to occasionally hustle other players. I particularly liked the games of 8-ball and straight pool. I have no idea how I would do today because I have rarely even seen a pool table since I was 17.

Eventually I found a summer job at a local lumber company that sold lumber and other building supplies to local contractors. It was labor intensive; I and a few other fellows unloaded boxcars and stacked lumber. Occasionally, once I learned where all the materials were located, I was allowed to wait on customers too.

As I entered my last year in high school, I elected to enroll in a course titled Distributive Education, which focused on business opportunities. The beauty of the course was that I could continue working at the lumber company for half a day during the school year and receive school credit for my work to count as part of the educational curriculum for the Distributive Education class. That meant I had a reliable source of income throughout my senior year because it doubled as work and study.

The company I worked for was extraordinarily forgiving and considerate of its employees. While unloading boxcars we often had to move them from one sliding door to another because the lumber was stacked by type and length and each stack had its own door opening for the lumber to be offloaded from the boxcar and stacked in its bin.

For instance, 1" by 8," 1" x 10," and 2"x4" all had their own doors and were stacked according to length. When we finished stacking 2"x4s" we might move the boxcar to another window to offload another size. To move the boxcar, we placed a fulcrum tool under a wheel and pried it to get the boxcar to move very slowly to the next window.

At an extremely slow pace the boxcar was easy to stop. However, one day I was in a hurry and I got the boxcar I was working on to start moving faster than usual. Little did I know at the time how difficult it would be to stop a boxcar that could weigh as much as 90 or 100 tons!

I could not get the boxcar to stop. I was putting 2"4s," 1"x 6s," and 1"x10s" under the wheels as fast as I could but the boxcar just chewed them up and kept on moving. Unfortunately there was a customer's car straddling the railroad track at the entrance to another company next door to our lumberyard, and when our boxcar struck that car it pushed the car up against the foundation of the other company's building and the car folded like an accordion.

I know the lumber company had insurance that covered it, but I also know they were upset about the accident. Yet the company executives never said a single critical word about it to me. They never took me off the job or criticized me for being careless. They just cautioned me to be careful about how I moved the boxcars.

Another time I was moving a loaded open bed 1924 truck from the railroad-loading zone to the interior of the company building where we stacked the lumber. The access road to the company was on a slight incline, and because of the heavy load I was carrying on the truck, I needed to shift gears on the incline. Unfortunately, there was a major traffic artery just behind the incline, and while I was shifting gears the truck rolled back about a foot.

Some of the lumber was sticking out of the back of the truck, and as luck would have it, as the truck rolled back a foot, a school bus passed directly behind me and a piece of lumber struck the bus window and imbedded itself in the bus. Nobody was hurt, but it was yet another incident for which I was responsible. Once more the company's insurance covered it, but I was very concerned about losing my job. The company was very forgiving and all I got was another lecture about being careful.

While I don't want to mention the name of the company, even nearly 60 years after those incidents I am still thankful for the experiences I had working for the folks who owned the company. I continued working for the lumber company throughout my high school year until I joined the U.S. Navy.

My grades were pretty unimpressive throughout high school. I finished with an average grade of 85.72, which by most standards is a solid "B" grade. I wasn't much interested in grades back then because I didn't plan on going to college. I was sure I would eventually join the Navy just as all but one of the men in my extended family had done.

I was so eager to join the Navy that in 1953, midway through my senior year, I tried to join, but I'll get to that in a moment.

By 1948, only three years after the end of World War II, as a product of the Cold War between the Soviet Union and the United States, Korea was split into two regions, with separate governments. Both governments claimed to be the legitimate government of all of Korea, and neither side accepted the border between them as permanent.

The warlike conflict between them began on June 25, 1950 when North Korea invaded South Korea. The United Nations, with the United States as its principal force, came to the aid of South Korea. China came to the aid of North Korea,

While it was not technically a war since none of the participants had declared war on each other, the casualties over the next two years were catastrophic. Historical sources put the full battle death toll on all sides at something nearing two million, although the figures are clearly not conclusive.

According to the Department of Defense the United States suffered 33,686 battle deaths, along with 2,830 non-battle deaths. South Korea reported some 373,599 civilian and 137,899 military deaths. Chinese sources claim the People's Volunteer Army suffered 114,000 battle deaths and 34,000 non-battle deaths, with 7,600 soldiers missing during the war. Chinese sources also claim the Korean People's Army suffered 294,000 battle deaths and more than 90,000 missing.

From my earliest memory I was sure I would eventually serve in the Navy. It had become somewhat of a tradition for men in our family to serve in the Navy and I didn't want to disappoint any of them.

The Korean War was drawing to a close and I wanted to be a part of it. So, with six months to go before my high school graduation, I ventured down to the naval recruiter's office and tried to enlist.

Fortunately for me, the recruiter explained that I would be a lot more valuable to the navy if I first finished high school. He literally talked me into returning to high school to hold off enlisting in the navy until after graduation. It wasn't what I expected, but it turned out to be one of the best pieces of advice anyone had given me up to that point in my life, and it would have serious implications for me in the years to come. The recruiter had explained to me how more valuable a high school graduate would be to the Navy than would be a high school dropout. His explanation made sense to me, so I returned to school.

Other people would have similar influences on me as I gathered life experiences over the next 40 years. Interestingly enough, it was a naval officer who talked me into going to college, a topic I'll cover in the next chapter.

Meanwhile two of my sisters had dropped out of school to marry their boyfriends. Both sisters immediately got pregnant and started raising a family, without ever returning to school. Their formal education stopped at about the eighth grade, but they lived reasonably good lives.

My oldest sister, who is only 11 months younger than I am, was married to three very different men over the years, all of who died and left her without any source of income. The truth is all three of them were deadbeats who never amounted to anything throughout their lives and she was never able to explain to me why or how she happened to fall in love with them. I knew that while she lived in Indianapolis, Indiana for a period of time, she had worked at an officers club and an Air Force colonel wanted to marry her, but unfortunately she wasn't interested in him.

She worked most of her life as a waitress in a variety of restaurants and raised a family—first in Indianapolis, Indiana, and later in Garden Grove, California, where she still lives with a modest income. Her primary source of income today is Social Security, plus a modest amount I provide each month.

We have loved each other and have maintained a very close relationship throughout our lives, and have always been able to have frank discussions about anything. Unfortunately we never lived close enough to each other for me to have much of an influence on her choices of men. Even today I live in Florida and she lives in Garden Grove, California, so we communicate every week mostly by emails and occasional telephone calls.

My youngest sister married a sailor who left the Navy and became a Mississippi riverboat pilot. He completed his nautical career as a pilot of the gambling boat that docked at an Alton, Illinois, pier where residents from the greater St. Louis area came to gamble and enjoy the ambience of a riverboat. He was and still is one of my favorite people whom I love dearly. He didn't have a college education but has always been very bright, sharp, and quick to see thorough scams and potentially bad experiences.

Unfortunately, his wife who was my youngest sister died at age 62 from COPD (chronic obstructive pulmonary disease) and emphysema. COPD is an obstructive lung disease that develops over time, typically due to long-term exposure of the lungs to cigarette smoke or other environmental irritants. When you have COPD, you may have one or both of the conditions that make up the disease—chronic bronchitis and emphysema. COPD makes it very difficult to breathe. It causes serious long-term disability and early death.

Despite many efforts, my sister was unable to give up her lifetime addiction to cigarettes. Even during the late stages of her disease, when it was terribly difficult for her to breathe and she had to have a constant source of oxygen, she still couldn't break her addiction. She had oxygen lines stretched throughout her house so she could have perpetual use of an oxygen tube. Still she couldn't break her addiction to cigarettes and would take off her oxygen mask long enough to smoke unfiltered cigarettes throughout the day.

Nevertheless she was a very talented seamstress who covered furniture to sell in and around Alton. She was a hard worker who was fiercely proud of her independence. She also raised four wonderful children, all of whom grew to be as independent as she was, and all of whom I love.

When she died, I was not able to attend her funeral or burial because my wife and I were touring Israel and my brother-in-law didn't know how to reach us. Even if he had connected with us, we would not have been able to return to the United States in time for those final moments

My third sister, who was the same age as my wife, loved to fish. One day in 1960, at age 22, she went down to the Mississippi River to fish in the early afternoon. Late that afternoon about 4:00 p.m. she came home complaining of a headache, so she laid down on the couch in our living room and quickly fell asleep.

Within two hours my mother noticed my sister was sweating profusely, so she woke her up. My sister said she really didn't feel good so my mother took her temperature, which as I recall was running well over 100 degrees. That was the first indication that something was very wrong with her. We decided to take her to the local hospital emergency room to see if they could figure out what was causing the high temperature.

The emergency room doctor checked her but couldn't diagnose a cause for the high temperature. He thought she might be coming down with a virus so he gave her some aspirin and sent her home, where she once more laid down on the couch and went to sleep. She continued to sweat profusely, and when my mom checked her temperature again, it was as I recall 104. I called my sister's doctor who was busy that evening serving as host at a party he was holding in his home. When I explained the problem with my sister he told me to "have her breath into a paper bag". That simply wasn't possible and seemed like a ridiculous piece of advice. I figured he was more interested in his party than in the care of my sister.

By 8:00 p.m. she seemed to be pretty restless, turning and tossing, so my mother tried to wake her to check her temperature again, but we couldn't get her to wake up. We didn't know it at the time, but she had slipped into a coma.

Unable to wake her, we called for an ambulance to take her back to the hospital. At the hospital they checked her temperature, which had spiked to a dangerously high level, eventually reaching 108 degrees, which they called hyperthermia. Her fever was literally frying her brain. They packed her in ice to try to break the fever, but it didn't work and by 11:00 p.m. my sister died.

The cause of death was hyperthermia, but even after an autopsy and inquest they could not determine the cause of the hyperthermia. She had gone from nearly normal at 4:00 p.m. to death seven hours later, and nobody was able to explain why she had died. I was angry with her doctor for not coming to her aid when I called him. He did respond to the hospital, but by then it was too late.

Even to this day, some 57 years later, we do not know what she might have contracted while fishing on the Mississippi River that could have caused such a quick and dramatic course of events. She had no prior history of illness that could have caused such a striking and precipitous fever. No one in our family had ever experienced anything remotely like whatever it was that took her life.

The consequence of her death was and still is that everyone in my family gets very concerned whenever one of us gets a fever over 100. My sister's death caused my mother to suffer from intense grief for several years. In fact I'm not certain she ever really overcame her inability to emotionally handle the sudden death of her daughter and the realization that we would probably never ever know the cause of the hyperthermia.

I assured mother that my sister's soul was in heaven and God will reclaim her body at the time of the "rapture." I knew that non-Christians would not believe in our Christian philosophy, but I also knew that it was at the heart of my mom's Christian belief system, and at that time she needed reassurance that my sister was in heaven. It was a particularly difficult time for all of us, because she was the first member of my immediate family to die, and we all loved her so much.

While my family's history in Alton stretched back to the 18th century, all but one of my siblings and I left Alton in the 1950s and are scattered across America. I live in Melbourne, Florida, my oldest sister lives in Garden Grove, California, and my brother lives in Moriarty, New Mexico. My younger sister was the only member of our family who remained in Alton. She loved the city and lived there her entire life.

I have only returned to Alton three or four times since 1953. Each time I returned I have been struck by the fact that it looks so quaint. While there are new sections on the outskirts, much of Alton still looks the way it did in the 1940s, except much older. When I returned for my 50th high school reunion in 2003, I remarked to a friend that the city looked familiar but very old, as though the foundations were weathering away but the buildings were still intact. I can only imagine how it will look the next time I return.

When I returned in 2007 for our 55th high school reunion there was a sea of gray hair. In some cases, there was no hair at all, or very little. Waists were thicker than I remembered, and everyone seemed shorter (the skeleton compresses over time). No one seemed to mind that we had changed so dramatically. There was no evidence of any disappointment or any form of the old status symbols.

The former jocks, beauty queens, cheerleaders and brainiacs just blended in. Everybody seemed genuinely happy to see everyone else, and that was a delight. Maybe it's because, after 54 years, no one has to impress anyone else. Whatever the reason, it was wonderful to see old friends and high school sweethearts reminiscing about the past.

I mention 54 years because we actually celebrated our 55th high school reunion during our 54th year because the organizers realized so many of our classmates were dying that they didn't want to postpone the 55th another year.

The truth is I hardly recognized anyone because besides the 50th anniversary reunion this was the only other one I ever attended. Those who attended a reunion every five years had no problem recognizing each other. I just didn't have that frame of reference, and almost nobody even resembled the faces I remembered

The fact that everyone looked old should not have surprised me. I don't know why I should have expected otherwise. The truth was that 125 of my 424 senior classmates had already died, and more than 10 were missing. When I returned again in 2007 for the premature 55th high school reunion, the number was even smaller. More of my classmates had died and fewer attended the reunion.

At any rate I haven't returned to Alton, even though organizers of our class reunions keep me informed when any more of our classmates die. Each time I receive a notice of the latest death it reminds me of the fact that I have already exceeded my own life expectancy. Life expectancy for men in our country is now

79, and I am already 82, well on my way to 83.

The changes in Alton were just as noticeable as the gray hair on the older students. There was an interesting blend of old structures with new and modern facilities. Some of the homes once housed Union soldiers during the Civil War.

On the bright side, the colorful floating casino, antique shops, Alton Museum of History and Art, Robert Wadlow statue, the Southern Illinois University campus, the legend of the Piasa bird, the return of magnificent eagles to the Alton bluffs, and the foliage, which is absolutely radiant with fall colors, offer tourist attractions that should provide a boost to the economy.

A bit of Alton history I neglected to mention is that the Alton area was home to Native Americans for thousands of years before the 19th-century founding by European Americans of the modern city. Historic accounts indicate occupation of this area by the Illiniwek Indians at the time of European contact. Archaeological artifacts discovered in the region demonstrated an earlier native settlement.

Much of Alton is located on bluffs overlooking the Mississippi River valley. Besides being beautiful, the bluffs protect Alton from yearly tornados that hit the bluffs and bounce off changing their course to hit other neighboring cities. The bluffs include an artist depiction of a Piasa Bird, which is a replica of what is alleged to have been a Native American dragon that is depicted in one of two murals painted by the Native American Indians on the side of cliffs above the Mississippi River.

The original Piasa illustration no longer exists; a newer 20th-century version, based partly on 19th-century sketches and lithographs, has been placed on the bluffs several hundred yards upstream from its original location. The limestone rock quality is not suited for holding an image, and the painting must be regularly restored.

Legend has it that the name Piasa is derived from the Native American word "Piasa," which was their name for "the bird that devours men" or "bird of the evil spirit." According to *The Legend of the Piasa Bird,* it was part bird, part reptile, part mammal, and part fish. Whether truth or simply legend, even to this day the Piasa Bird fascinates visitors to Alton.

Other than work, my high school years were actually pretty uneventful. I wasn't a jock and had no athletic skills that I knew of, although I was to learn later in life that I had considerable athletic potential I didn't know about as a youngster.

I'll discuss that in chapter 4. I didn't participate in any notable high school programs other than Distributive Education and had no extraordinary personal or family experiences other than the ones I have already described.

While I didn't know it at the time, the Midwestern and Christian values I learned at my mother's side and from my hometown experiences would serve me well throughout my life. After high school graduation my next adventure was in the U.S. Navy.

CHAPTER 2
LIFE IN THE U.S. NAVY

As soon as I graduated from high school, I returned to my local naval recruiter's office and enlisted in the navy. Even though the recruiter also handled recruitment for the Marines, I was not interested in joining the Marines mostly because so many men in my extended family had already served in the Navy. It was considered a tradition that men in our family serve in the Navy.

The Army and Air Force didn't appeal to me because, except for one uncle on my mother's side of the family, whom I didn't know very well, no one else in my family had ever served in the Army or Air Force. Also, that uncle didn't volunteer for the military; he was drafted into the Army. The Air Force didn't interest me because it was still struggling to establish its own reputation since it had been part of the Army for so many years and didn't become a separate and independent military service until September 18, 1947. As far as I was concerned, the Air Force didn't really come into its own until the 1960s when we entered the space age seriously. Then the Air Force became the glamorous service, and I considered it again. But, I'll cover more on that later.

In 1953 all I knew about the Air Force was what I gathered from 1940s movies, such as the Howard Hawks movie *Air Force*, with John Garfield and Gig Young, *30 Seconds Over Tokyo* with Spencer Tracy, and *Twelve O'Clock* High with Gregory Peck and Dean Jagger (one of my favorite movies, incidentally). Movies like those depicted the Army Air Forces in World War II, but didn't do much to promote a career in the modern newly formed independent Air Force. So, off I went to the Navy!

Keep in mind I had not yet been any farther than 50 miles from Alton. My first surprise was that I was assigned to the Navy Recruit Training Center (Boot Camp) located in San Diego, California, instead of the one in Chicago. Joining the Navy and immediately going to San Diego was little more than a fantasy to me. I didn't know anyone who had ever actually been to California. Just the thought of going to San Diego was almost as exciting as joining the Navy.

The Navy paid for a bunch of us recruits to travel from St. Louis to San Diego by train. Except for occasionally watching a train pass through Alton on its way to or from Chicago, I had never even seen the inside of a passenger train. With my meager income stream, if I had to pay for travel to San Diego, it would have been by Greyhound bus, so I looked forward to travelling on a train.

Most of us Midwestern recruits had never travelled so far, especially in the comfort of a passenger train. Much to my surprise, most of the guys got together almost immediately and started playing cards. They clearly weren't as excited about train travel as I was.

They weren't playing canasta or pinochle either; mostly they played poker, and I was aghast at how much money changed hands. I had never seen so much money piled in stacks on a table, and I wondered how these guys made the kind of money they were losing.

I didn't then and I don't now gamble, but I was fascinated by how much money the recruits seemed to have. I figured they hadn't come from the same kind of poor background as I had. I was nearly broke and wouldn't have any more money until my first Navy paycheck. I sure wasn't going to risk losing the few bucks I had by playing poker.

Other than gambling, the trip to San Diego was uneventful, but the scenery we passed was fascinating. San Diego is 1,853 miles from St. Louis, and I had no idea how far that was or how long it would take to get there. I just knew I was on an exciting new adventure.

As I recall, it took us three days to travel to San Diego and I remember thinking we were beginning to be a bit ripe by the time we arrived. Even in the best environment, three days without a shower pushes the envelope on personal hygiene. We could shave every day, but the Navy didn't pay for private compartments and three days of communal living wasn't the best way to make an instant impression at boot camp.

The Naval Training Center at San Diego had its beginning in 1916 with 278 acres donated by the San Diego Chamber of Commerce and the City of San Diego. Over the years it expanded to its present size of 435 acres. The base was so large it looked like a small city to me, and the architecture was unlike anything I had ever seen in the Midwest.

I had never even imagined so many beautiful and colorful buildings, surrounded by Palm Trees, and had never seen orange roof tiles. The weather was magnificent, and it was the first time I had ever been close enough to see an actual ocean that was not in a movie. It took me several days to quit looking at the beautiful environment of that new world.

When we first arrived we were given thorough medical and dental exams, various mental tests (which I always suspected were designed to measure our intelligence) and were issued various outfits of naval uniforms and clothing, none of which fit very well, except for the shoes. The shoes made sense because if they didn't fit well, it would mean blisters and really sore feet.

About 70 of us were "welcomed aboard" by James E. Emley GM1 (Navy First Class Gunner's Mate), an impressive petty officer who represented the Naval Recruit Training Center's Commanding Officer. Before his assignment to the Naval Recruit Training Center, Petty Officer Emley had demonstrated leadership abilities over years of naval service and had received special training on how to work with naval recruits.

We were then assigned to Company 194 and Petty Officer Emley stayed with us throughout our training. He was considerate and inspirational, while being demanding and strict at the same time. He was well liked and respected by most of the recruits I knew. At that point in my military career, as a seaman recruit (a one-striper), a first class petty officer seemed like a very high rank that came with a lot of respect.

I later learned that the battery of tests we originally took helped the navy establish which career field we would be assigned to when we graduated in 12 weeks. I also learned that it didn't really matter how I scored on those tests; once the Navy discovered that I was a proficient typist they decided my career pattern would be in the Yeoman career field, and I would have nothing more to say about it.

When I originally joined the Navy, I had thought I would like to serve in some capacity in the Construction Battalion (CBs). After all, I had taken auto-mechanic, woodworking, and machine shop courses throughout high school, and it seemed logical that I would fit into the CBs. None of that mattered. As far as the Navy was concerned, as soon as they found out I was a proficient typist, they decided I had a ready-made skill set that would be perfect for the Yeoman career field and that was where they pegged me from the moment they discovered I could type. I didn't really mind because I had always liked to type. From the time I first sat down at a typewriter, I was comfortable with it and developing a skill with it came naturally to me.

In the modern American Navy, yeomen perform administrative and clerical work, operating office equipment like typewriters, word processors, computers, and fax machines They also answer telephones, sort incoming mail, organize files, and do all manner of office writing, including business and social letters, notices, and reports.

In addition, yeomen perform office personnel administration, maintain records and official publications, and perform administrative functions for legal proceedings, such as preparing briefs and other documentation. An equivalent civilian job to yeoman would be an office manager or administrative assistant.

As unusual as it may seem, in high school I had taken two semesters of typing classes and became one of the best typists in those classes. I could accurately type nearly 90 words per minute on a non-electric standard typewriter. I was the only boy in both classes, and I took a lot of grief from male friends for developing skills in what they considered to be a girl's area of expertise. Male friends constantly asked me if I planned to become a secretary when I graduated from high school. Little did they know!

As mentioned earlier, I had also taken an assortment of male-oriented courses, but nothing ever served me quite as well in life as learning to be a proficient typist. Everywhere I went after high school, good typists were in short supply. You could always find "hunt and peckers," but reliably good typists were valuable to almost any office.

What I later discovered throughout life was that typing was one of the most important skills I ever learned. It came in handy throughout my professional life and is still one of the most important skills I have. I typed my own master's thesis in graduate school, all of the more than 500 articles I've had published in newspapers and magazines around the world, and the four books I wrote prior to this one. I have continued to use my typing skills virtually every day of my life. Later, during another period of my life, I even taught my wife how to type and how to be a proficient secretary.

Having shipped our civilian clothes home and donned our new Navy uniforms, we began a rigorous training schedule that I discovered would involve marching as much as anything else. We marched everywhere we went, whether to the chow hall for meals, the drill sites for exercise, the classrooms for instruction, or to medical facilities for tests and exams. We marched until many of us felt like our legs were going to fall off, and then we marched some more.

I would learn that marching was one of the important ways the Navy taught us how to work together as a unit. After a while, once my legs got into shape, I began to enjoy the marching. There was a rhythm to it, and I could hear the cadence in my head, sometimes even after we quit marching. But there was a lot more than marching to learn during that 12-week program.

While it's true that training includes classroom indoctrination on the rules and regulations by which the Navy is governed, naval history, traditions, customs, and the responsibilities a sailor assumed as a new member of the Navy, it also taught us about the Navy's rank structure and its system of career advancement.

We learned how to recognize the various naval ranks and ratings, which were considerably different than those of the Army, Marines, and Air Force, and the opportunities we would have to attain petty officer or commissioned officer status. At that point in my life I had no idea what the difference was between a petty officer and a commissioned officer. They all looked impressive to me as a raw recruit.

I learned about the nature of serving on ships, how to use small arms, such as the Browning automatic rifle, the Thompson sub-machine gun, a variety of ordnance, and larger guns such as a five-inch and 40MM guns using dummy ammunition. I was surprised at how good I was with firearms since I had very limited experience with anything remotely like the weapons we learned how to fire.

My experience with weapons had been with a 410/.22 Over and Under shotgun I used to hunt rabbits. A 410/.22 over and under was a combined 410 shotgun with a .22 caliber rifle. It was a Remington model SPR94 over/under combination rifle/shotgun. A 410 Bore/.22 Long Rifle caliber had a 24-inch barrel and a three-inch chamber with a two-round capacity. I had never handled a pistol until I joined the Navy, but I was fairly proficient with the 410/.22. I loved that rifle, but even today I can't remember whatever happened to it once I left home.

Nevertheless, I became very proficient with pistols, especially the standard military .38 caliber and .45 caliber pistols. For some unknown reason I scored well with these pistols. Even today I am still good with a pistol, although today I have a Walther PPK/S .380 caliber (9 MM short), double action, semi-automatic pistol. In fact, that make and model has been in existence for over 130 years and is the weapon of choice for James Bond in the movies. It is light, fairly small, easily concealable and storable.

We also learned how to use a gas mask, oxygen breathing apparatus, and other equipment designed for personal protection. I must admit that I don't remember much about the things I learned in that class, but I do remember we spent an entire day learning about it.

Almost all of the information we learned was useful because most people who make a career of the Navy spend many years of their service on ships at sea, so knowledge of basic seamanship is fundamental. A lot of time was spent learning the language of the sea and how to use Navy tools, such as the marlinspike, knot tying, steering and sounding, anchoring and mooring, as well as how to recognize various types of ships.

We also learned some of the fundamentals of damage control such as principles of fire fighting and a working knowledge of the equipment that might be required to save our ship and the lives of our comrades.

To learn most of these basic skills we used a land-based almost full-scale model of a destroyer escort for practical exercises. It was such an accurate replica of a ship it looked as though the Navy had transported it from the sea to land just for our training.

By the time we completed our training, we had learned many of the fundamentals of seamanship and how to find our way around a modern ship. However, a lot of our training was outside the classroom and involved physical and military training, which is to say it involved learning how to keep our bodies physically fit and how to work together as a unit. Some of the recruits were far from physically fit, and the physical training was designed to "harden" our bodies and get them ready for more physical stress than many of us, especially those of us who were not athletes, had ever experienced in civilian life.

To build some of us up and trim some of us down, and to condition all of us for the rigors of life at sea, a well-planned physical training program was integrated with other phases of training. It included strenuous physical exertion through lots of calisthenics, instruction in swimming and sea survival, and instruction in first aid, lifesaving, and personal hygiene.

Actually, I didn't need any swimming instruction. I have been a good swimmer all of my life, although I once put my life in jeopardy in the Philippines, not because I couldn't swim adequately, but because I exercised poor judgment. I'll get to that later.

In addition to calisthenics, we played many team sports such as softball, basketball, volleyball, and a sport none of us had ever heard of called flickerball.

Flickerball was originated in 1949 at the University of Illinois. It is a combination of basketball and football and is played with a regulation football on a field that is 80 yards by 30 yards. It is an outdoor game that is played by two teams of seven players, but any number may play. The object of the game is to score a goal with an overhand pass thrown through a mounted plaque with an opening in the center from at least 15 yards away

A player may not run forward with the ball toward the goal. He may run sideways or backwards but cannot advance the ball. He can only advance the team by passing the ball forward. If a player catches the ball on the run, he may take three steps to stop or lose possession of the ball to the other team. The ball cannot be held for more than five seconds or the person holding it will lose possession of it to the other team. Once more, the object, like almost everything we did was to promote teamwork. To win at flickerball a team must be well-integrated and coordinated.

Most of all, military training taught us the importance of strict obedience to orders and the importance of the individual in a military group, whether he is on land or at sea, whether he is working in an administrative capacity or as part of a gun crew, fire crew, or standing duty on the bridge. I would later learn that to be truly effective, everyone on a ship must pull together as a team.

I remember thinking the most important lesson we learned was how to live together as a group. Most of us had lived alone or at home with our families and didn't have to worry about how to take care of our clothes, how to keep them clean, or how to take care of our living quarters, all of which can be dramatically different experiences for a young man. Personal accountability became singularly important to us, especially during inspections when an individual's faulty performance could penalize his entire unit.

If the drill non-commissioned officer couldn't bounce a quarter off our beds, we would spend overtime working on the bed instead of going on liberty in downtown San Diego. If one individual failed the inspection and his entire unit was punished with a denial of liberty, you can guess how that went over with his teammates.

In addition to learning all the formal matters the Navy includes in its program, a major part of recruit training is simply learning how to adjust to an environment that may be quite strange to a new recruit. That environment can include bullies, racists, sissies, crybabies, malcontents, and a mix of personalities the like of which we may never have seen during our civilian lives. For instance, a racist recruit from the south quickly learns that racism is not tolerated in the Navy or in any other branch of the military. A racist may not like someone from another race, but he must quickly learn to respect and work cohesively with that member, at least while in the work environment.

I had never met anyone from the Deep South before boot camp and was not prepared for the racial slang I heard from other white guys or how they assumed every other white guy shared their opinions of black sailors. It was a shock that took some adjustment to decide who among my classmates was worth trusting and developing as a friend. My mother had always taught my siblings and me that in God's eyes everyone was the same, and He loved us all. Prejudice was not allowed in any form in her house whether it took the form of racism, ancestry, weight discrimination, or any other form of slight. With mom, it was very simple, God loves everybody.

I remember a guy from Meridian, Mississippi who had a really wonderful personality, was warm and friendly all the time, except when the subject of race came up. He made it clear that he thought blacks were inferior to whites and didn't look forward to serving with black sailors. He had to hide his racism as best he could during boot camp, but after boot camp I always wondered how he adjusted to the real Navy.

A recruit gets up early and goes to bed late. He can be tired all the time but must still perform the physical demands of marching, drilling, and physical training. The single most important adjustment tool for me was knowing for certain that the Navy and my fellow recruits could do anything they wanted to me and demand any kind of performance, but they could not stop time.

It was a simple concept. When the 12 weeks were up the nonsense would stop and we would get a new rank and a new assignment in the real Navy. All the harassment and all the stress would end in due course; we just had to be patient and meet the Navy's training standards, after which we would have to adjust to new stresses in a real world work environment.

Meanwhile we could put up with anything they threw at us. I kept reminding my new buddies of that, especially those who were having a hard time adjusting to our new adventure. And a few recruits simply could not adjust to the new regimen. I could hear several of them crying at night in their bunks. A few of them had such a terrible time adjusting that they were literally kicked out of the Navy and sent home. Keep in mind we were all volunteers, not draftees.

I bided my time waiting for a new assignment. I kept my space clean, my bed made properly, my uniforms squared away, paid attention in classes, followed orders religiously, performed whatever physical demands were necessary, scored well on the firing range, was a standout in group exercises, and generally went unchallenged while I waited for my new assignment.

After a few weeks we were allowed to go downtown to San Diego on liberty. I didn't participate in liberty often because I didn't have much money to spend and I wanted to send home some of what I had. Besides, I was so tired all the time I didn't much feel like going downtown. I preferred to take naps, feeling like there would be plenty of time for liberty after graduation from boot camp.

I was ecstatic when I got my new assignment to a naval base in Sasebo, Japan. I couldn't believe my good luck. Some of my friends got assignments in the United States and felt lucky to stay close to home, but I was hoping to get something overseas. Japan sounded so exotic and exciting, I could hardly wait to "ship out." For me, on that day the "sound of success" was completion of boot camp as we stacked arms and received our orders for a new rank and a new assignment. I no longer had one stripe on my sleeve; my new rank was seaman apprentice and it included two stripes. It wasn't much, but it was the latest "sound of success" for me.

For my new assignment I would have to travel to Japan aboard a troop transport ship. It would be a long trip, about 14-days as I remember, with a new and exciting beginning. There would be lots of us travelling for the very first time, cramped together on a large naval troop-carrying ship.

I learned very early the difference between a boat and a ship. Lots of civilians call naval ships boats, but a boat is a vessel that can be carried aboard a ship. Boats are used to carry sailors from their ship to shore. Ships carry lots of boats. No sailor would ever think of calling a ship a boat.

I wasn't expecting the sort of ocean trip we faced. We shipped out on a troop transport that left San Francisco for our 14-day trip across the Pacific Ocean. There seemed to be thousands of us, although it was probably more like a few hundred. The ship was nice enough, but two days out from San Francisco, we hit rough waters and all of us green recruits got seasick. I can still remember it. There is nothing quite like the feeling of nausea that comes with seasickness and the perpetual feeling that you need to vomit.

Seasickness is a form of motion sickness, and virtually anyone can be subject to seasickness. It relates to your spatial orientation that tells your brain what's happening. It involves your inner ears, your eyes, skin pressure receptors, and muscle and joint sensory neural receptors. What that means is an individual gets seasick when the brain receives conflicting messages from the four symptoms. Perhaps your eyes sense no motion but your inner ear tells your brain you are moving violently.

The first telltale signs of seasickness are often lethargy and a slight drowsiness, followed by a nauseous feeling and a cold sweat. These symptoms can increase and the face can become paler, sometimes even greenish. It becomes difficult to concentrate on a task. The nauseous feeling can become uncontrollable and may lead to violent vomiting. Even the thought of food, especially greasy food, compounds the problem. All in all it's a very unpleasant experience.

Eventually your body adjusts to the nauseous feeling and you get over the seasickness, but it can take days. Meanwhile it is a miserable feeling.

The regular crew was constantly laughing at us and some of them would walk around holding a bucket with a fork over it carrying a greasy pork chop, which tended to make sick sailors even more sick. All over the ship I could hear the sounds of sailors vomiting and moaning. It stayed that way for about three days until we began to get our sea legs.

That was almost the last time I ever got so seasick, but I never forgot what it felt like, and I was always sympathetic to guys who had to endure several days with their heads in a toilet. If you aren't sick along with everyone else, you may become sick from the stinking smell of vomit everywhere. I never understood how the ship's crew could avoid the affect of watching and smelling everyone else who was sick, and it seemed evil to me that they would compound the problem with their greasy pork chops.

Once we arrived in Japan we were quickly processed and given new assignments. The US Fleet Activities Sasebo is a naval base located in southern

Japan. The base serves as a focal point for forward-deployed units and other visiting units of the US Pacific Fleet and designated tenant commands.

The US Fleet Activities Sasebo hosts the surface fleet of the Japanese Maritime Self Defence Force and US Navy under a bilateral relationship between Japan and the United States. The base supports the Seventh Fleet of the US Navy to maintain peace and security in the Pacific region.

For the first three months, with a new rank of seaman apprentice I worked in the fleet post office sorting mail and performing whatever general duties my supervisor assigned to me. When we went to the train to pick up our sacks of mail, we carried a side arm, which was a standard Colt .45 revolver. Later I would learn that the standard sidearm for the military was usually a .38 pistol. It didn't matter to me because I was pretty good with either of them. It never occurred to me that anyone would try to steal sacks of mail, but it was my job to help guard the guys who were carrying the mail.

Meanwhile, we lived in a floating barracks tied up to a dock. We shared living quarters that included bunk beds and storage lockers for our clothes and valuables. Few of us spent any more time there than necessary because Sasebo on the southern island of Kyushu was the first place most of us had ever been outside of the United States, and it was so interesting we wanted to spend as much time as possible exploring the local city, which most of us found to be wonderfully exciting. If nothing else, everyone I knew was fascinated with the variety of Japanese food choices. It was an experience I remember even today.

The noticeable difference was that while I was not old enough to be served liquor in the United States, there was no corresponding restriction in Japan. They were quite willing to serve me liquor anywhere I went, so it was not unusual to have a drink or two while on liberty. Of course I occasionally over indulged, but that too was a lesson I needed to learn. Showing up for work with a hangover was frowned upon, and I was careful to not do so very often.

I was pleasantly surprised to find that despite the fierce reputation of the brutal Japanese military during World War II, those we met in Sasebo were invariably very friendly, polite, and accommodating. We delighted in observing the Japanese culture, which was so alien to most of us. It was and still is a culture in which older people are revered and respected, and families take care of their elderly. This is very different than what I observe in much of the United States where older people, particularly the infirm, can be treated like a nuisance.

I can honestly say I saw no evidence of the rude and violent Japanese nature that was so evident in American movies and newspaper articles during World War II. Stories brought home by Americans who had been prisoners of war in Japan, and books about the Japanese occupation of places such as China, particularly the *"Rape of Nanking,"* has even to this day left the impression that the nature of Japanese soldiers is unthinkable brutality. The Japanese had a long history of a warrior class that created a brutal mindset.

According to the History Channel, perhaps the best example of Japanese brutality occurred in late 1937. Over a period of six weeks, Imperial Japanese Army forces brutally murdered hundreds of thousands of people in the Chinese city of Nanking, including both soldiers and civilians. The horrific events are known as the Nanking Massacre or the Rape of Nanking, because between 20,000 and 80,000 women were sexually assaulted. Nanking, then the capital of Nationalist China, was left in ruins, and it would take decades for the city and its citizens to recover from the savage attacks.

Also, the History Channel records that after the April 9, 1942, United States surrender of the Bataan Peninsula on the main Philippine island of Luzon to the Japanese during World War II (1939-45), the approximately 75,000 Filipino and American troops on Bataan were forced to make an arduous 65-mile march to prison camps. The marchers made the trek in intense heat and were subjected to harsh treatment by Japanese guards. Thousands of the prisoners perished because of Japanese brutality in what became known as the Bataan Death March.

In the United States I have sometimes met retired military officers and enlisted men who served in the Pacific during World War II who even today speak about their terrible experiences with the Japanese. Those who were prisoners of war in Japanese camps can be very descriptive of the way they were treated as POWs.

But the Japanese citizens I met were genteel and courteous and made me feel welcome. While I was in Japan I saw absolutely no evidence of a brutal nature in the Japanese citizens.

Nevertheless, I can't help but wonder if the Japanese military ever goes to war again whether they might revert to the kind of behavior for which they were known internationally, especially in China and the Republic of the Philippines, during World War II.

These are some of the real questions, for which I have no answers. Did all

Japanese have a brutal nature during World War II or was it just the military. Do Japanese citizens inherently have the genteel nature they display now or are they merely sublimating their brutal nature because they lost the war? At any rate I saw nothing of that brutal nature during my time in Japan.

After three months working in the fleet post office, I was transferred to the fleet motion picture exchange, only a few blocks from the post office. The fleet motion picture exchange was where designated representatives from ships that were temporarily docked in our area would come to pick up movies that could be shown aboard ship while they were at sea. When they returned to port, they would bring back the movies that had been shown and pick up new ones for their sailors. Nobody in the fleet knew it, but we saved the best movies for submarine crews who always showed up with presents like canned hams to exchange for the good movies.

The problem, however, was that movies that were shown at sea often came back with watermarks on the filmstrips from splashes at sea. So we had to screen every returned movie to make sure it was not too damaged to issue to another ship. One of my jobs, when I wasn't issuing films at the main counter, was to screen movies in the back room to ensure they weren't too damaged to reissue.

That meant on some days I might have to watch three or four feature films back to back, which sounds like an easy and perhaps enviable task. For those of you who think so, I suggest you try to watch three or four or five movies every day for a week to see how you feel about such a job. After awhile I reached a point where I didn't care if I ever saw another movie for the rest of my time in the Navy.

For several years after that assignment I never went to movies. I had so much movie trivia stored in my brain that I could give curious individuals unending details about current movies. For instance, if you gave me the name of a movie I could give you a detailed synopsis of the plot, a list of its stars, and what year it was issued. If you just knew the name of a star that was in it, I could give you the name of the movie and a synopsis of the film along with its running time.

In succeeding assignments folks were fairly impressed with my movie trivia ability, and often suggested I try to get on a television game show, forgetting how difficult that would be while serving aboard a ship at sea. It turned out my assignment to the naval base at Sasebo, was just a weighing station between assignments.

After a bit over six months I was assigned to Commander Service Division 31

(COMSERVDIV-31), which was a rotating flagstaff commanded by an admiral that stayed at sea for long periods. For instance when the ship on which the flagstaff was serving rotated to the United States, we just moved our entire staff aboard its relieving ship.

My first COMSERVDIV-31 assignment was aboard the *USS Bryce Canyon (AD-36)* a Shenandoah-class destroyer tender. The function of a destroyer tender or a repair ship was to serve as an auxiliary ship designed to provide maintenance support to a flotilla of destroyers or other small warships. Those destroyers would line up next to the destroyer tender while conducting maintenance.

On September 26, 1953 the *USS Bryce Canyon* sailed for Sasebo, where she arrived on October 16, 1953. Thereafter, the *USS Bryce Canyon* rendered tender service in Sasebo, Yokosuka, Nagoya, and Kobe during this tour. She returned to the United States on June 17, 1954.

Our next assignment was aboard the USS Jason, a repair ship that served in the western Pacific from November 6, 1953 to February 1955. The *USS Jason* departed Oakland, California, on July 22, 1950 for Sasebo, and immediately began service duties upon her arrival in August. Throughout the Korean War, she remained at Sasebo for extended periods performing the repair tasks at hand, with only brief overhaul periods in the United States. Following the cessation of hostilities in Korea, the *USS Jason* returned to San Diego, on November 6, 1955.

We then moved to the *USS Ajax (AR-6),* a Vulcan-class repair ship and the fourth ship in the United States Navy to bear that name. On her 1953-1954 cruise to the Far East, *USS Ajax,* in addition to her operations from Sasebo and Yokosuka, participated in the two-month operation "Passage to Freedom" supporting a group of U.S. Navy ships sent to carry refugees from the Hanoi/Haiphong area of Communist North Vietnam, down to Saigon. During this operation *USS Ajax* was stationed at Touraine, Indochina, a French port that later became Da Nang, South Vietnam. I joined the ship while it was visiting the Republic of the Philippines enroute to Vietnam.

You might well wonder what I did while serving aboard these three ships. I performed routine yeoman duties, typing, filing, and doing any other administrative duties that our supervisor, a Navy lieutenant, equivalent to an Air Force captain, directed.

The Navy lieutenant, whose name I cannot remember, offered me the next best piece of advice in my career progression. He was so impressed with my work that he took me aside one day and said to me: "You have far too much potential to continue in your present career path. You need to get out of the Navy at your first opportunity and go to college. You have far too much potential to sit behind a typewriter all day. "Once you get your education, you can always return to the Navy and get a commission. A Navy career as a commissioned officer can be far more rewarding than anything you can achieve in you present path." Needless to say I was impressed and extremely grateful for his confidence and I took his advice to heart. It would come in handy some years later.

During our break time several of my friends and I played pinochle—a card game routinely played by four people. My buddies and I played pinochle almost all of our spare time, except when we were ashore on liberty. When we had to return to work, we would leave our pinochle hands in place on our table and return to the same game on our next break.

While serving aboard ship for a short period in the Philippines I often took liberty and went swimming in the waters off Subic Bay. The naval base at Subic Bay was a major ship-repair, supply, and rest and recreation facility located in Olongapo, Zambales, Philippines.

As I mentioned earlier I was very good swimmer. However, one day, without thinking much about it, I swam out about one-half mile against the current. Unfortunately, while swimming out, the tide changed so when I turned around to return to the beach I was still swimming against the tide. It was the most difficult swimming struggle I ever had before or since that episode. I got so tired I wasn't sure I could ever make it back to shore. It seemed to take forever, but I eventually did make it back. Even so, it was a terrific lesson about making sure you know what you're doing before you attempt those things. I have never tried anything like that since. The fear of overextending myself has kept me in check ever since that swimming experience.

While the *USS Ajax* ship was temporarily visiting Subic Bay, I was transferred to the *USS Pinola (ATA-206)* which was operating from Sasebo, Japan. So back to Japan I went. The *USS Pinola* was a Sotoyomo-class auxiliary fleet tug launched in 1945 and serving until 1956.

The *USS Pinola* was the last ship I served on during my naval career, but it was probably the most memorable of all my assignments. The ship was small by most standards. According to the Navy's web page on this ship, it was only 143' long, with a 33' 10" beam, a draft of 13' 2" and a maximum speed of 12 knots, although most of the time we cruised at eight knots.

The crew was also very limited with five officers and 40 enlisted men. The captain was a "Mustang" lieutenant commander who worked his way up through the enlisted ranks. Its armament was meager: a single 3"/50 caliber dual purpose gun mount and two single 20mm AA gun mounts.

It was not fast, but it could pull its weight in gold. It had two diesel-electric engines and a single screw. We pulled a barge three times our size from Midway to Hawaii in 1955, but I'll get to that later.

I joined the crew of the USS Pinola in Sasebo, where it was temporarily operating in the waters off South Korea from August 2, 1954 to March 27 1955. Its principal purpose was to tow target sleds for surface gunnery exercises for the Fleet Training Group based at San Diego. It was also capable of retrieving surface mines, although we didn't retrieve any during my tenure aboard her.

The gunnery exercises were interesting to say the least. We would tow a target sled one mile behind us and ships such as destroyers and cruisers would sit three to five miles away from us and fire their guns at the target sled. A reasonable distance on either side or behind or in front of the sled would be considered a direct hit. I forget the distances but they were something like 50 yards in front or behind and 100 yards on either side of the sled would be considered a direct hit. It was not supposed to actually hit the target sled, which was expensive to repair or replace.

The sled had its own radar on which the shooting ship was supposed to fix its guns. Unfortunately on one exercise I recall that the cruiser that was firing scored a direct hit and blew the radar off the target sled. Without even knowing it, the next shots were fixed on the radar on our ship and shells began to drop around our ship. I can still recall hearing our skipper as he grabbed the mike with which he was communicating with the shooting ship and without even the pretense of protocol he just yelled "Knock that shit off. We're going home." That was the end of the exercise for that day.

One day off the shore of South Korea was particularly memorable because of the weather. We were in a storm that developed into a typhoon, and we took a 51-degree roll. The ship was supposed to capsize at 49 degrees, but for some unknown reason we righted again and rode out the storm. The consequence of that weather was that everyone aboard our ship, including "old salts," were heaving their guts up. There was no such thing as having sea legs in that storm. We all got seasick.

After that, in 1955 we began our trip back to our homeport of San Diego.

Before we began our trip to San Diego, I had been promoted to yeoman third class, a petty officer rank. When the promotion came through, it was part of the ship's promotion tradition for the crew to throw overboard those being promoted. I thought I had escaped the tradition because I was working below deck, but I was wrong. Several of my crewmates found me, picked me up, and carried me outside and unceremoniously threw me overboard. It was a well-intended and fun exercise, but I still got pretty banged up from trying to fight them off, which was also a tradition. Not only was I unsuccessful, but also I had bruises everywhere to show for the effort, theirs and mine.

Our return trip to San Diego was memorable primarily because it took so long. On a stop at Midway, we were given a few hours off for free time, and many of us decided to go for a swim right at the dock. Some of us decided it would be fun to dive off the ship into waters around the side of the ship.

My first dive from the bridge, which was near the top of the ship about 30 feet from the water, was anything but pretty. I had never dove from such a high position and didn't allow for the height, which meant that my legs wanted to flop over so I had to really arch my back to keep from landing on my back when I entered the water. I arched it so much I could hear popping sounds. Fortunately I didn't break anything but that was the first and last time I ever tried to dive off the bridge. My back was sore for several days.

Just before we departed Midway for Hawaii, we were hooked up to a barge with a truly heavy load of sand to pull to Hawaii (I know, how insane it sounds to tow sand from Midway to Hawaii). Our ship had an enormous screw that made it possible for us to pull really big loads. We couldn't move very fast, but we could tow almost anything.

All in all it took us 37 days to travel from Sasebo, Japan to San Diego, California. I had to stand a four-hour watch every eight or 12 hours (I can't remember anymore the exact spacing of time). It was my job to stand watch above the bridge, keeping a sharp eye out for other ships, whales, or anything else that might interfere with our course.

Of course I don't think I ever saw anything during the entire trip, except for one sighting that later embarrassed me. I reported that I had sighted a ship off to our starboard side about a mile toward the horizon. It soon became clear that what I thought was a ship was actually a large whale sounding (blowing air out of its lungs as it exhales). Everyone got a good laugh at my expense.

Standing watch was dreaded duty because it was dull. It was so tiring watching the horizon through binoculars. At times it seemed like we would never cross the ocean. I can't even explain how beautiful Midway and Hawaii looked as we pulled into their ports.

The beauty of the *USS Pinola* was that it was a dungaree navy, which meant that any time we were at sea, we wore dungarees in a very informal environment. Class "A" service-dress uniforms were for use in port. As soon as we left port, the skipper put on a baseball cap and dungarees and we didn't see a navy hat until we got to the next port. Also, while at sea he often fished and caught some truly beautiful fish, which the ship's chef would prepare and share with the crew.

Speaking of food, we ate well, as you might expect of a dungaree navy. We didn't have trays. It was our tradition to eat on plates with real silverware, and our chef was an extraordinary cook. For the year I was on that ship I never heard anyone complain about the food, which is quite rare in the military.

The chef was also pretty resourceful. I often watched him try to ferment fruit in jars in the mess because alcohol was not allowed on the ship. I don't think he was ever successful, but he kept trying.

My job was to look after the crew administratively. I was the only yeoman on the ship, which meant I was responsible for processing everything from recruitment, re-enlistments, discharges, promotions, liberties, leaves, maintaining individual service records for every crewmember, and anything else that required administrative paperwork. I was very popular because I was the only source for this kind of administrative support.

We finally arrived in San Diego where we resumed pulling target sleds behind us so naval ships in the area could get gunnery experience. I fell in love with San Diego and loved to go downtown on liberty. In fact I kept a locker downtown with civilian clothes I could change into on liberty so I wouldn't be instantly recognized as a sailor. Of course, you know how unsuccessful that was, but I was a naïve young sailor.

At that point I was still not 21 and would be 'carded" any time I tried to buy an alcoholic drink. I had been used to being served in Japan without anyone caring how old I was, but in San Diego it was always a problem. So, I grew a mustache, which added a couple of years to my image, and I never again had any trouble with being "carded." I also didn't drink often because I didn't want to risk going back to our ship inebriated, which is a fancy word for drunk.

I also started taking dance lessons at the local Arthur Murray Dance Studio and would attend dances at the local YMCA, from time to time, so I could find potential dance partners. That was another reason to not drink alcohol. I did not want to show up at the YMCA with the smell of booze on my breath. Those dance lessons came in handy for many years after I left San Diego.

Meanwhile my time in San Diego passed quickly and shortly after I arrived there I received orders to the Pentagon where I was assigned to a branch of the Office of Naval Intelligence. It was yet another new experience for me. In 1962 the *USS Pinola* was transferred to the Republic of Korea, but that ship will always occupy a special place in my memory.

When I arrived in Washington, DC, I was assigned to live with many other sailors in a barracks located about two blocks from the Pentagon on Columbia Pike, a major artery in Arlington, Virginia on which the barracks no longer exists today. The barracks was simply called Quarters "K." It was really handy because it was a just a short walk to work.

All we had was a bunk bed and a locker in which we kept our clothes and other valuables. There was also an enlisted "club" on base for sailors, men and women alike, to socialize and have non-alcoholic drinks, except for those who were over age 21 who could drink whatever they wanted. We spent a lot of our off-duty time at the club rather than go downtown because it was a fun environment and the drinks were cheap. Besides, we had a lot of female sailors stationed there too, and I got to practice the dance steps I had learned while in San Diego. A new friend of mine, another yeoman, was an excellent dancer, and he taught me great dance steps I didn't know. He would teach me new steps in the barracks, and we would then go to the enlisted club and try them on unsuspecting girls.

Regrettably none of that barracks and club area exists today. Quarters "K" and the enlisted club as well as the entire support base was demolished to make way for the widening of U. S. Highway 95 that passes through Virginia on the way to Maryland. Anyone driving there today would not even be able to tell a base was once located on Columbia Pike to support sailors who worked in the Pentagon. I have no idea where sailors assigned to the Pentagon live today.

Now there are about a dozen traffic lanes, including U.S. 95, that empty into a four-lane 14th Street Bridge across the Potomac River. Whoever designed that little piece of highway history made a huge mistake. Leaving Washington, DC on U.S. 95 can take as much as an hour to get across the 14th Street Bridge because of backed-up traffic.

While assigned to the Pentagon I attended a briefing on the new highway passing by our building. I asked why there never seemed to be enough roads to accommodate the traffic. The briefer replied that no matter how fast they build or improve highways they are always behind the growth rate. They just can never seem to get road construction out in front of the traffic build-up.

For those who have never visited Washington, DC, or otherwise don't know about the Pentagon, here is what life was like there 60 years ago, which is different than it is today. The building is the same, but access to it is quite different.

At that time, in late 1955, the Pentagon was the most impressive building I had ever visited. In fact, it is still the most impressive building I have ever seen. I have visited 35 countries on five continents, and I have never visited any other building anywhere in the world that comes even close to the awesome majesty of that building. It is in my opinion beyond comparison.

For those who are not familiar with the Pentagon, it is the headquarters of the United States Department of Defense and is located in Arlington County, Virginia, across the Potomac River from Washington, DC. It is the international symbol of the United States military, and the outside of the building is frequently shown in major motion pictures and television shows, even those that have absolutely nothing to do with the military or national security.

It's like focusing a movie camera on the Empire State building in New York City just to emphasize the location of the film when that building has nothing to do with the movie.

According to the Department of Defense, the Pentagon was designed by American architect George Bergstrom and built by general contractor John McShain of Philadelphia. Ground was broken for construction on September 11, 1941 and the building was dedicated on January 15, 1943. Until you've been there, it is impossible to appreciate how impressive it must have been to see that building go up in 16 months. Today it can take nine months just to build a modest house.

With 6,500,000 square feet of space, of which 3,700,000 square feet are devoted to offices, and approximately 23,000 military and civilian employees, plus 3,000 non-defense support personnel, it is one of the largest office buildings in the world. The population of people working in the Pentagon rivals many smaller sized cities across the United States.

According to *The Pentagon, Facts & Figures* it has five sides, five floors above ground, two basement levels, and five ring corridors per floor, with a total of 17.5 miles (28.2 km) of corridors. The Pentagon includes a five-acre central plaza in which many employees buy and eat their lunch. It is shaped like a pentagon and informally known as "ground zero," a nickname originating during the Cold War on the presumption that it would be targeted by the Soviet Union at the outbreak of a nuclear war.

According to a Pentagon Memorial Dedication, on September 11, 2001, exactly 60 years after the building's construction began, American Airlines Flight 77 was hijacked and flown into the western side of the building, killing 189 people (59 passengers and the five perpetrators on board the airliner, as well as 125 victims in the building), according to the official report. It was the first significant foreign attack on Washington's governmental facilities since the British and Canadians burned down the city during the War of 1812.

According to the History Channel, it's difficult to understand just how big the Pentagon is. It is twice the size of the Merchandise Mart in Chicago and has twice the office space of the Empire State Building. The U.S. Capitol building could fit into just one of the building's five sides.

It is so big it is easy for anyone to get lost in it until they learn the physical layout of the building. When Dwight Eisenhower assumed his position as Army chief of staff after World War II ended, he got lost in the vast complex while on a walk and was forced to ask a group of stenographers for directions back to his own office.

However, even though the Pentagon is roughly a mile in circumference, anyone who is familiar with its layout can get from the two furthest points in under 10 minutes by taking a shortcut through the open courtyard at the center of the complex (Ground Zero), and by walking very fast. For those unable to physically walk the corridors on their own, the Department of Defense provides a fleet of scooters, or self-propelled vehicles, that are allowed to zip around at up to 3 mph. When I worked there I had no trouble getting around the surface five sides and concentric rings, and could easily find snack bars where I could eat.

On the other hand, there are two basement levels that are not so well laid out. It was and still is quite easy to get lost in the basement because there are no identifiable points of reference similar to those above ground. More than one time while I was stationed there I got lost in the basement and had to call someone to lead me back to the surface.

In 1955 the Pentagon, like most government buildings in the Washington, DC area, was open to the public. Anyone in the world could just walk in and leisurely stroll through its halls. Once the layout is understood, navigating the halls is quite easy, and it was not unusual to run into unescorted visitors all over the building. Of course, at any given time some of them were lost too.

The Office of Naval Intelligence is America's premier maritime intelligence service and a core element of the U.S. Navy's Information Warfare Community. Much to my surprise, as the sole yeoman on a Navy tugboat, I didn't expect to receive an assignment to a prestigious naval intelligence office in the Pentagon.

The office to which I was assigned, which was a branch of the Office of Naval Intelligence (Op-923R), was responsible for keeping the naval attaches around the world supplied with equipment they needed to do their jobs. It may not be well known that the principal job of attaches is to gather intelligence information for the United States embassies. It was our job to make sure they had the equipment they needed to help them collect intelligence information.

To do that my office had a huge innocuous storage room full of cameras, listening devices, and other information-gathering tools that helped the attaches gather information. My job was to keep tract of those devices and supply them to the attaches whenever they needed them.

Some of those electronic devices are probably still being used today, although more refined with greater capability, so I won't describe any of them. Just believe that intelligence-gathering devices and tools have become very sophisticated over the years and are capable of gathering complex and sensitive information that helps our government carry out its national security missions.

I considered that assignment to be the highlight of my brief naval career. I know other people in our office had other duties, but I was proud of being the source of equipment to help our intelligence officers gather important data.

When I was discharged from the Navy in the fall of 1956, I would continue serving in the inactive naval reserves until 1961. At the time of my 1953 enlistment the United States had a Universal Military Training and Service Act that required all men to serve a total of eight years in military service in any one of a variety of ways, as long as the active duty and reserve years served totaled eight years.

I enlisted under what was called a Minority Cruise Service Program that required me to serve until one day before I turned age 21 after which I continued to be carried on the inactive reserve roles until I had completed eight years, which of course meant they could recall me to active duty any time during those reserve years, much like they do today with reservists who are sent to Iraq and Afghanistan.

Combined with the 12 weeks I would later serve as an enlisted trainee with the Air Force while in the Officer Training School program I eventually had eight years, two months and 28 days of enlisted service.

While serving at the Pentagon, I had been active in a local "little theater" program and had been bitten by the acting bug, which fascinated me. So I thought I would look into the prospects of attending college, as my Navy lieutenant supervisor had recommended in 1953. The only difference was that I had no intention of returning to the Navy. I knew that anyone making a career out of the Navy would spend a lot of time at sea away from his family. While I enjoyed my sea duty experiences the thought of spending 10 or 15 years at sea didn't have much appeal for me.

Contrasted with civilian occupations, the military divorce rates can be very high because of long family separations and difficult reunions when the spouses are reunited. While the figures change over time, in the 1960s the Navy's divorce rate seemed to be higher than the other services, principally because sailors spend so much time away from their families, and reunions after a long separation can be very difficult.

While the husband is away from home, the wife becomes the sole provider of support and discipline for the family. It is not always easy to give up that role when the husband returns and sometimes its causes friction in the marriage that cannot be resolved. Besides, while I was not married and enjoyed my sea duty experience, the idea of returning to the Navy in any capacity did not have much appeal for me.

My experience with the community theater in the Washington, DC area left me thinking about the possibility of becoming an American actor. I had enjoyed my introduction to Community Theater so much I began to think about the prospects of pursuing theater professionally, especially acting.

I was young and naive and had no idea what the odds were against anyone starting from scratch to become a successful actor. So I did some research and was shocked by what I discovered. The movie industry was represented by the Screen Actor's Guild, which had more than 100,000 members. The problem was that fewer than 500 of them seemed to be working at any one time. It just seemed to be a huge gamble, particularly if one is married, but I was single and willing to risk whatever it took to succeed in that new field.

Meanwhile I discovered that very few graduates of the Southern Illinois University's (SIU) theater department even tried to become professional. Most of them worked as school teachers or entered some other profession. But as naïve as I was, I just thought that was a personal problem they would have to deal with. It wasn't something that I needed to contend with, so I was willing to give it a shot.

Even with outrageous odds against success, the thought of becoming a professional actor had great appeal for me, so when I got home I checked out the communications program at Southern Illinois University (SIU), which was known to have a great program with emphasis on theater. I simply was not discouraged by the depressing statistics.

After sending for a university brochure I visited the SIU campus to learn about the theater department. I discovered a small theater with a stage that had fairly limited space, but professors who were enthusiastic about their programs.

I liked the rest of the campus and the local community where I would eventually live. But I still had some reservations about the importance of a university education, so I went back home to think about it. That meant if I wasn't going to school, I would have to find some kind of work to support myself until I finally decided what it was that I wanted to do. Meanwhile, I would give a lot of thought to attending the SIU theater program while I was working.

While home I took a job at the local Luer Brothers Meat Packaging plant that carved up cattle and hogs for commercial outlets such as grocery stores.

I started out as a laborer working with hogs. The hogs were butchered on an assembly line process. They were strung up on hooks by their legs, their throats were slit so the blood could drain out of them, then dipped into a vat of scalding water to singe off the outer hair, and then processed along a route that included individual stops for focus on specific parts of the hog's body.

For the first day I was a singer. Mine was the third stop where I stood on a platform as the hogs came out of the vat of scalding water. It was my job to use a blowtorch to singe off the hair that wasn't lost in the vat of water. Later along the assembly line different people butchered and packaged the hogs,

As the hogs progress along the assembly line, scrapings, blood, and guts fall onto the floor under the assembly line, and another employee scrapes up the mess and takes it away. Part of the day, I was relieved of the singeing blowtorch job because my hands, legs, and back became so sore. It was difficult for me to stand up. The cleanup job under the assembly line was even more tedious, because I spent so much time bent over. But the worse part was the smells. While the hogs were being slaughtered, the smells outside of the plant were enough to make ordinary citizens turn up their noses, but the odors inside the building were terrible for a while. However, I was amazed at how quickly I got use to them. After a while I found the smells outside the plant to be worse than those inside. I never did figure out how that happened; I just accepted it.

Only one week at the meat packing plant convinced me that a university education was a great idea. I could not see myself working in the meat packing plant for much longer, so I quit and returned to the university to gather more information.

SIU was and still is located in Carbondale, Illinois, about 95 miles south of St. Louis, 120 miles south of Alton in a region informally known as "Little Egypt," and about 65 miles north of Paducah, Kentucky.

According to historians there are two schools of thought on how this southern tip of Illinois became known as Little Egypt. The first holds that the regional name developed because of the existence of Egyptian place names such as Cairo (pronounced Kay' Roh) and Thebes. The second argument states that the region was named after settlers in the northern part of the state who had to travel to southern Illinois to buy grain after a series of bad winters or droughts. The settlers in their wagon trains were similar to the ancient Israelites traveling unto Egypt to buy grain. Both probably represent a little bit of truth, but neither has anything to do with SIU. I include the information simply because I think it's an interesting part of history about the area in which SIU sits.

After a return trip to SIU and two days of looking over the campus, I registered as a student, which was not difficult because unlike regular students, there were no requirements for veterans to meet. Then I returned home to Alton, packed my bags, and drove to Carbondale to begin the winter quarter of study. At that time, unlike most other universities, SIU was on a quarter system instead of a semester system.

As I recall the tuition and cost per quarter hour was fairly low, certainly nothing like the cost of going to college today. I might be off a bit, but the point is that it was a whole lot cheaper than it is to go to school today.

Today SIU is on a semester system and the cost depends on how many credit hours the student carries, plus other fees associated with on campus attendance and whether the student is an Illinois resident.

I was lucky because I had the benefit of the GI Bill that covered a lot of my expenses. It wasn't enough to live on but it was great financial help. It might actually be the best reason for having joined the Navy when I did.

I also discovered there were lots of unused scholarships lying fallow that for some unknown reason students didn't seem to apply for. I immediately applied for and was granted an academic scholarship that paid a small stipend as long as I maintained a "B" average. I no longer remember the dollar amounts, but combined with the GI Bill, that scholarship helped a lot. Still, I worked throughout my undergraduate college years, and graduated without having a college debt to repay. Today, many college graduates amass huge financial debts that they struggle for years to repay, partially because college tuitions have become so expensive and partially because they are supported by their families and don't work while attending college.

A few of my older friends who didn't have any financial help worked full time and attended school full time while they were also raising a family. I didn't envy them because it was clear they were having a difficult time balancing all of their family issues along with the demands of college. I noticed they also had a tough time keeping up with their assignments and grades. But most of the veterans I knew were plodding along as best they could, balancing the requirements of school and family.

After my experience at the meat packing plant, I was absolutely thrilled to be going to college.

CHAPTER 3
SOUTHERN ILLINOIS UNIVERSITY

I started courses at SIU in the fall of 1956, its first full year as a university. It had previously been a teachers college for 87 years. It has since grown to become one of Illinois' largest and most well known and well-respected universities. It is now the flagship campus for a diversified multi-disciplined university with multiple off-campus locations around the state of Illinois, as well as extension course opportunities around the United States, and even around the world.

In 1956 there were about 3,000 students and had growing pains as it expanded to become a university. Nobody was quite sure how the former teacher's college would grow into a university concept, but I wasn't concerned about it. The proof of concept is that today there are about 30,000 students on its main campus and other locations around the state.

In addition to its reputation for high academic standards and diversity, the Carnegie Foundation for the Advancement of Teaching ranks SIU among the top 5 percent of all United States higher education institutions for research. The SIU faculty is well-known for its standing in the world of research. It is home to numerous successful research specialties.

SIU has a competitive program that is open to all disciplines. It offers up to 20 grant awards each year to full-time SIU-Carbondale undergraduate students to work on an independent research project, creative activity project, or both, with a faculty mentor.

And, from my perspective, it had and has an outstanding theater department where I expected to get a lot of technical knowledge, coupled with a lot of acting experience.

Since I had already registered for school, my first task was to find somewhere to live. I was older than all of the other students I had already met, and being a military veteran, I did not want to live in a school dormitory with a bunch of undisciplined teenage kids with the kind of insane problems I had heard about fraternity life. That meant I had to find somewhere in town to live.

As luck would have it I found a home about two blocks from campus and a half-mile from the SIU theater department in which a really nice older widow or divorcee, I don't remember which, was renting rooms to college students. She had a three-bedroom house and was renting out two bedrooms, with two students in each room. She occupied a bedroom, kitchen, and major bathroom, and we all shared the living room, although we students didn't have much use for the living room.

Another student who didn't stay there long after I arrived already occupied the room I rented. He was having academic problems and eventually dropped out of school. I was told he flunked freshman English three times. I was glad he quit because he was a bit of a teenage slob who just dropped his clothes on the floor in our room, and I sometimes had to step over them to get to my bed or closet. He was not the kind of roommate I wanted.

Luckily another veteran soon occupied the room with me, which meant we would be suitable roommates because of our ages and common military experiences. It turned out that all of my three roommates were really nice guys who shared a desire to get an education and return to a work environment.

Actually, other than the military, my primary roommate and I didn't have a lot in common. He was going to major in business, and I was going to be a communications major with an emphasis on theater. He was also a jock who wanted to try out for the SIU baseball team, and I didn't have any athletic abilities that I knew of. Much to his disappointment, even though he was the fastest runner from home plate to second base, and was really good with a glove and bat, when he tried out for the baseball team, he didn't make the cut. He was unbelievably disappointed, but that is reality and he was mature enough to adjust quickly to his frustration. After his initial disappointment I never again heard him comment on the fact that he had not made the cut.

The other bedroom was rented by another business major and a rock (geology) major. They too were veterans. So my introduction to school was off to a good start.

I was starting college in the winter quarter, which meant I had already missed the fall quarter. My first day in school I immediately visited the SIU theater department, where I would spend a majority of my time during the next four years.

The university campus was large and beautiful, with lots of new buildings built to accommodate its new status as a university.

The SIU Department of Theater, which is what the university calls it, offered a combination of theory, practice, and imagination—an effective blend of academic work, production experience, and creativity, with lots of opportunity to study acting. It was just what I wanted.

While it was more modest in 1956, today the theater department is housed in the Communications Building on the southwest corner of the university in a large beautiful building with an incredible theater. The theater resources at SIU are spectacular. Named after one of my favorite professors, Dr. Archibald McLeod, the former chairman and founder of the Department of Theater, the McLeod Theater is a 521-seat, fully-equipped proscenium arch theater with a grand drape. The stage is 60' wide and 40' deep. Side stages with sliding doors embrace the right and left sides of the proscenium and can be opened to expand the panorama for an additional 20' on each side.

An arc shaped apron 15' deep and 40' at its widest point is equipped with an automatic hydraulic system and can be lowered to create an orchestra pit or a variable-height playing level. A counterweight balance and rigging system allows scenery to fly into the 50' fly gallery. The theater is fitted with a computerized lighting system, with LED lighting instruments and an audio system with a back-of-the-house sound booth.

A fire curtain allows the apron and front of the house to be separated from the stage area. Seating is tiered with a Continental styled lower level and a tri-sectioned upper level.

It is the kind of theater that gives students every opportunity to learn in an environment that will prepare them for working in a professional theater or for teaching in an ideal educational environment. It is the kind of theater every serious actor would relish.

It combines the advantages of a large university experience with the personalized attention of smaller colleges and the excitement of a fully functioning theater production company. It is now and was then just what I had hoped for. However, it is grander today than the theater complex that existed in 1956, when I first became an SIU student. But since I had never been to another university and had nothing with which I could compare the SIU theater department, I was suitably impressed with the old school, the old theater, and the existing faculty. It was too soon to be impressed with any of the students, but I would learn that many if not most of them would not take seriously the great opportunities the SIU theater department offered.

Dr. Archibald McLeod was a bit older than other faculty members I met. He was born in Edinburgh, Scotland, on November 5, 1906 and came to the United States in 1920. He came to SIU in 1947 and taught in the Speech Department while also staging plays. In 1956 he became the first chairman of the newly created Theater Department, where he developed courses on acting, directing, playwriting, dance, set design, costuming, and makeup.

McLeod served as chairman for 17 years. He organized summer repertory theater companies, touring companies, and a children's theater program. In 1962 and 1966, he took students to Greenland and Iceland to perform for servicemen at military bases. In 1969 he helped establish The Center for Soviet & East-European Studies in the Performing Arts at the SIU campus. He was instrumental in establishing theater program opportunities beyond the confines of the university campus.

In 1971, 1972, and 1974 the Theater Department's performing company performed in the American College Theater Festival in Washington, DC. While at the SIU campus, McLeod started the country's first national intercollegiate scene design competition and played a role in bringing professional scenic designer Mordecai Gorelik to campus as faculty. Dr. McLeod was the consummate professional who established a new theater department from scratch and saw it develop over his tenure into a world-class theater program.

He retired from SIU in 1975 and became the first executive secretary of the Illinois State Theater Company. He later helped found The Stage Company in Carbondale in 1982, where he continued to design sets and direct plays. He died on April 6, 1992.

I mention these details about Dr. McLeod because while I studied at SIU he was my absolute favorite professor and played a huge role in teaching me stage presence, which I would later use in my professional business positions. I will never forget the hours he worked with me to perfect my cockney accent for *She Stoops To Conquer*, which I will discuss later in this chapter.

On my first day as I stepped through the entrance to the theater, which was considerably smaller and much less impressive than the present facilities, and walked down to the stage area, I could see that students were dismantling the set for a play that had just finished. Since I had begun my education during the second quarter of the school year, I had missed the first play of the season, which was *Arms and the Man*, a comedy by George Bernard Shaw.

The theater and the building that housed it were quite small contrasted with its present facility, but it served us well, seating about 300 people. From my limited theater perspective it was impressive, even though the facilities were really rather modest.

When I got to the stage, two sets of legs were sticking out from under the bottom of the set, but I couldn't see to whom they belonged. Two people were obviously dismantling the set. A bit later when they emerged from the set I was introduced to a very pretty girl named Peggy and another student she was dating who would become my first roommate for a brief period.

I met a lot of theater majors that day, most of who did not impress me as people who were serious about working professionally in the theater or entertainment industry. Most of the people I met seemed to think theater was something they might dabble in but not something they would take seriously.

My first few months on campus were spent familiarizing myself with the campus generally and the theater department specifically. I also checked with the university registrar's office about the kind of scholarships that might be available. I was attending school on the Korean GI Bill but that wouldn't pay for all of my expenses. I would have to find work on campus or in town to carry me through college and I thought it might help since I also qualified for a scholarship.

I don't remember how much the scholarship paid, but it couldn't have been more than a modest stipend; but combined with my other sources of income it would help cover my expenses.

There were lots of jobs available on campus, but I discovered I could work for the theater department and be paid a modest amount of money doing general maintenance work. Dr. McLeod was very receptive to having a more mature veteran helping instead of an inexperienced young student.

One day, after several months, my roommate, who was the one dating Peggy and who it turned out happened to be a bit messy, told me he and Peggy had a falling out, and he wasn't dating her any more. I told him if he wasn't dating her I was going to ask her out to see if she would date me. By then I had met her several times in the theater department, and I thought she was vivacious, interesting, and beautiful. I couldn't imagine what attracted her to my roommate, but I didn't care as long as she was available for me to invite on a date.

I asked her out and she said yes. Much to my roommate's surprise, that was the end of him and the beginning for me. I dated Peggy throughout my freshman and sophomore years and fell madly in love with her almost immediately. She had a personality quite different from that of any other girl I had ever dated. Her personality was also very much different than mine. She was an extreme extrovert and a flirt, but that didn't bother me mostly because none of it appeared to be serious. I was an introvert but as seems to be so common in our society, opposites actually do attract and it was no different with us. We seemed to hit it off very quickly.

I was immediately attracted to her whimsical and contagious personality. I had never dated anyone quite like her. For me she was a breath of fresh air. She was three years younger than I was and lived with her sister and brother-in-law in Herrin, a small city about 20 miles east of Carbondale.

She claimed she was attracted to me because I was a veteran and was more mature than other eligible guys. The truth is there was a strong attraction between the two of us and I loved to spend time with her.

We didn't just hang out at the theater department. SIU had a magnificent library where we could study. The library was a quiet place where we could sit for hours in a small cubicle holding hands and listening to classical music as we studied. It was difficult for me to focus on anything else when I was with her.

Morris Library is the main library for the SIU-Carbondale campus. It holds more than 2.6 million volumes, 36,000 current periodicals and serials, and more than 3.6 million microform units. It also affords access to the statewide-automated library system and to an array of electronic sources.

The SIU web site points out that the Morris Library is the heart of SIU's educational commitment. That's a formal way of saying the library offers everything a student could possibly need in the way of library support.

In my junior year, after about a year of dating, I proposed marriage and she said yes. I have always believed choosing Peggy to be my wife was the smartest thing I ever did in life. I'll cover more on that later.

During my first year in college I was introduced to some theater professors I genuinely liked and a lot of very bright theater students. Even some of those who didn't take theater seriously were quite bright. They just didn't see theater as a serious topic. There were basically five professors in the theater department in

1956. Today there are 13 professors, plus two emeritus faculty members, and several staff members.

The two founding professors included Dr. McLeod, and Dr. Sherwin Abrams a theater department faculty member. They seemed to run the department jointly. They didn't of course, but that was the way it looked to me initially.

I quickly established a relationship with both of them and enjoyed working for them as a part-time employee and learning from them in classes they taught and plays they directed. Most of all I enjoyed getting acting parts in their plays.

Later I would meet Dr. Christian Moe who taught playwriting and Darwin Reid Payne whose specialty was teaching and practicing scenic design. Dr. Moe arrived late in my university experience, and I only had one playwriting class under him. He was interesting and very creative. Darwin Payne was a brilliant designer of stage sets and a genuine artist. He left teaching and went to New York City to try to break into professional stage design but for some reason he didn't stay long.

He eventually returned to SIU and continued teaching his courses in scenic design. I considered his return to SIU to be an advantage for our student theater majors. All of his work was unbelievably impressive to me, and I enjoyed watching him create sets. It was like watching an artist at work. In fact all five of the theater department faculty members were excellent teachers.

During the course of my SIU education, I had virtually no interest in other departments. I had to take other academic courses, such as algebra, botany, English composition, and an assortment of other subjects that didn't interest me to meet the school requirements for graduation. I took a lot of liberal arts courses along with a spattering of science and math courses, and never got good grades in any of them.

The truth is that during that period I just didn't care about those courses and didn't study them. I received a straight "C" average in the academic courses while making "A" in most of my theater courses. I've since found it interesting that I've never had to use anything I learned in those other courses. For instance, I've never ever had to use anything I learned in algebra or botany. If they didn't somehow involve a form of communication, I did a minimum amount of work just to get the mediocre grade, but my major focus was on theater, particularly acting. I was being cast in a lot of plays, getting very good grades and a lot of experience.

During the course of my four-year theater department education, I participated in every play the theater produced, either as an actor, stage manager, technical assistant, or stagehand. It would take entirely too much space to review all the plays and parts I was involved in by name. Suffice it to say there were many and I loved them all.

I was fortunate enough to audition for and be cast in a variety of diverse characters in many plays from which I developed a well-rounded base of experience as an actor. I also learned a lot about how to stage-manage a play and how to create sets from scratch. I simply fell in love with theater and communications generally.

While my communications major focused principally on theater, I had to take several of speech courses too, all of which were great learning experiences that helped me to become more comfortable in public speaking environments.

In the corporate world it quickly became evident to me that many corporate executives could benefit from taking public speaking courses. I learned that most of them had a great storehouse of technical knowledge but were not very good at communicating their knowledge to less knowledgeable people.

My years at SIU were somewhat idyllic. After the pressures I experienced in the Navy and the distasteful experiences working in the meat packing plant, college seemed like a vacation with study. For me a college assignment was just a suspense I had to meet for creating papers to generate grades. I noticed that for some students assignments were just a distasteful chore that they often neglected. I was always eager to get any kind of assignment in the theater department.

I had always been a good reader; so studying seemed more like a pastime than a job, and left plenty of time for me to date Peggy, which I loved doing. We shared an interest in theater that made every date an opportunity for fruitful discussions about our classes and acting experiences, not to mention that I just loved being around her. I treasured her laugh, and she made me smile in ways nobody else was ever able to do. In truth my interest in Peggy was second only to my interest in theater and eventually those two interests would flip-flop.

It did not take me long to fall in love with her. As an aside, I can tell you that I have loved her for 61 years, and I have never ever been seriously interested in another woman since the first date I had with her. Her personality has fascinated and intrigued me ever since we first dated, and it still does today.

I am embarrassed to admit that after meeting Peggy I didn't treat other women as kindly as I should have. I remember one time I had another date I had made with a student before I had met Peggy. The night of my date with the other girl I knew that Peggy was visiting a friend of ours that evening, so I cut short my time with the date and took her home early so I could rush over to my friend's house to be with Peggy. That was really poor judgment that could not have made my date feel good about her or me. It was a rotten thing to do, and I felt bad about it for a long time afterward, but if I had it to do over, I would probably do the same thing. I was so enamored with Peggy that no other woman interested me.

The problem I had with the other students in the theater department was that I had spent years in the Navy where everyone took their jobs seriously, and it bothered me that so many students seemed to approach their study of theater like it was an elective course that just filled a blank on their schedule, or something they might do as a hobby once they graduated. I wanted everyone I met to see theater as something more important than an elective course to fill out a college degree.

The truth was that I was an anomaly, the odd man out. I treated my university work just as I had my jobs in the Navy. Any job worth doing was worth doing well. That means approaching every task as though it is supremely important. I saw college as an important path to my future, not some frivolous investment in a social experiment or some extracurricular activity to pass the time in between classes.

Only one other student seemed to be as serious as I was about making a career out of acting. Years later I discovered he had done just that. He had gravitated to Hollywood after graduation, got the right breaks and for many years he had made a living as a Hollywood character actor in the movie industry. I won't mention his name for fear of embarrassing him.

His biography describes him as a ruddy, red-haired, burly-framed American character actor of the '60s and '70s often as a brash blue-collar or volatile villain. He was a very good character actor who made an excellent living in Hollywood.

Over a long career in Hollywood he played characters in far too many movies to mention. He also appeared in 52 television shows where he created reoccurring characters in television series such as *Gunsmoke*, *Murder She Wrote*, *The Rockford Files*, *Fame*, and *Ellery Queen*. Another reason I don't want to mention his name is because he eventually developed an alcohol problem, was involved in an automobile accident in which three people were seriously injured, and spent 28 months in a California prison for drunk driving.

He is now retired and no longer involved in the movie business. But he was a well-known character actor for many years. At SIU we appeared together in several plays and some years later got together a couple of times in California, but after he retired from acting he moved away from the Los Angeles area and we lost contact. I haven't seen him for many years, which is unfortunate because I really liked both he and his wife. He was a brilliant storyteller and could hold an audience in the palm of his hand even at a cocktail party. He was also an excellent father who took care of and had a loving relationship with a disabled son. I later learned he had anticipated I would gravitate toward Hollywood and become an actor too.

During my first two quarters at SIU I mostly took courses that satisfied some of the academic requirements to graduate, along with one or two theater courses. The third quarter, which was the summer of 1957, I participated in a theater department course that included three months in a summer theater program at the Kelso Hollow Theater, a major outdoor amphitheater near Springfield, Illinois.

SIU's summer theater program granted 12-quarter hours of academic credit to students who participate in the program. About 15 actors and actresses from coast to coast, but mostly from Illinois, gathered in New Salem, 20 miles northwest of Springfield, to pump new life into the Land of Lincoln with their repertory performances in the park's 300-seat, open-air theater.

From an acting standpoint it was an invaluable experience because of the diverse acting opportunities, being able to create new characters every week in different plays. It also offered a marvelous opportunity to socialize with and get to know how other serious participants viewed the entertainment industry.

Of course the days were long and tedious because when we were not studying our lines we were constructing sets for the next play. I would discover later that there was little difference between participating in the university summer theater program and a professional summer stock program, which I participated in the next year.

The local community residents were used to having a theater group in their area during the summer months. Since the theater was basically located in a state park, lots of visitors would stop by to look over our facilities during the day. Unfortunately many of them went home toward the end of the day instead of staying for the evening show. Nevertheless we always had lots of interested patrons in the audience, and I think we appreciated them as much as they appreciated us.

The experience was so exciting that the three months of summer went by in a flash, and when we returned to campus, the newer theater department students were impressed with the experiences we had that would not be available to them until they were able to take the same course the next year. It gave us a bit of gravitas with other students in a way that would not otherwise have been possible. The summer experiences exceeded my every expectation.

SIU no longer participates in the summer theater program at Kelso Hollow Theater, because the SIU Department of Theater now offers a summer program on its Carbondale campus at the McLeod Summer Playhouse. It is a season of professionally mounted productions through June and July, featuring a company of young professional performers gathered from auditions across the United States.

The summer season concludes with the All Southern High School Theater Project that offers an opportunity for area high school students to work with professionals in the university's theater, jointly produced with Carbondale Community Arts, which I consider to be an excellent opportunity for local high school students to get first-hand knowledge about the theater.

The next quarter, the fall of 1957, was even more exciting because I was selected to participate in another curriculum experience not generally available at other universities. SIU offered a "theater practicum" course that involved participation in a three month touring theater in which about a dozen students toured southern Illinois with a single play putting on shows in community theaters. It was a delightful experience that was unlike anything students could get in the theater department on campus. It offered a range of different audiences for our play every day, and it was not always possible to anticipate the reactions of audiences from different communities. The extra beauty of the program was that the university granted participants 12-quarter hours of academic credit.

We travelled to cities all over the southern part of the state, putting on a play titled *She Stoops To Conquer*, an 18th century English comedy of manners written by Oliver Goldsmith and first performed in London in 1773. The play is a favorite for study by English literature and theater classes in the English-speaking world. It is one of the few plays from the 18th century to have an enduring appeal, and is still regularly performed today. It has been adapted into a commercial film several times in recent years available to mass movie audiences. If the movie ever plays in a movie heater near your neighborhood I highly recommend you see it.

The part I played was that of Tony Lumpkin, a delightful part that required that I learn to speak in cockney, a distinctively lowbrow accent and dialect that occasionally uses rhyming slang. Of course the beauty of only playing one part over a three-month period is that there was lots of time to develop the part, with more shading than can usually be created during a short-running show. Dr. McLeod, the theater department chairman worked with me for weeks to develop the cockney accent to a more believable degree and I had a lot of fun with the character.

One of the most enjoyable experiences of the touring schedule during our three-month road trip was a stop at Menard Correctional Center, which used to be known as Southern Illinois Penitentiary. It was located about 50 miles southeast of St. Louis. Most of us had never visited a penitentiary and we didn't know what to expect at a maximum-security prison housing more than 3,000 prisoners.

The prisoners turned out in mass, filling a large recreation center, and it turned out to be our very best audience throughout the three months tour. The prisoners didn't have a lot of opportunity for our kind of entertainment. They laughed loudly, applauded after every scene, and generally showed us how much they enjoyed having us visit their facility. They may well have shown as much pleasure for any visiting group, but we never doubted their sincerity and appreciated their response to our performance. Besides, it gave us a perspective of prisoners that none of us had ever expected.

Another interesting aspect of the touring theater was that I had been selected by Dr. Sherwin Abrams to be the comptroller for the theater group, which meant that while we were on tour, I made all of our meal arrangements, selecting different restaurants, after which I paid all of our bills and kept a record of expenses.

Selecting the restaurants and hotels in which we would eat and stay overnight was an interesting experience because I had to deal with different individual tastes and preferences and could not make everyone happy at the same time. When we departed I paid all of our bills, and each week when we returned to campus I would give an accounting to Dr. Abrams. The job paid a modest amount for my effort, which helped me with personal expenses. To tell the truth I actually enjoyed being the comptroller and would probably have done it for nothing if they hadn't paid me to do it.

When the three-month tour ended, our play ran for two weeks on the SIU campus. Our reception on campus was almost as exciting as it had been by audiences on the road. Dr. McLeod again worked with me for days to perfect my cockney accent until it was even more believable, which was just delightful for me and for the audiences.

I remember how gratifying it was to hear the audience laughing and clapping as I left the stage at the end of my scenes. It always surprised me that the audiences would applaud every time I exited the stage. I would learn that it was a sign of their great approval of my cockney accent. They enjoyed hearing it as much as I enjoyed creating it.

It gave me an appreciation for what motivates professional entertainers. For those who have never acted on a stage, one cannot imagine what a wonderful feeling it is to have an audience demonstrate in a very positive way how much they like your performance. There is almost nothing like it anywhere else in life.

I haven't used cockney since 1957 and have no idea how I would do it today. I generally have no ear for regional dialects or accents. It has been more than 60 years since then, and I don't remember anything Dr. McLeod taught me about speaking cockney. I suspect it is the same for professional actors who must learn to mimic different accents for different parts and then forget those same accents once the part is complete.

Somehow it never seemed right to get 12 hours of academic credit for doing something that was so much fun, but I would learn that my experiences from the summer theater and touring theater would pay off well with knowledge that would be applicable in later courses and stage productions for the next two years of college and, as it turned out, for the rest of my professional life (I'll discuss that more in chapters 4 & 5).

In the spring of 1958, as incongruous as it might seem following three months of summer theater and three months of touring theater, in addition to a couple of required courses that had nothing to do with theater, I took a course that was titled Introduction to Drama, a required course for my major. It was anti-climatic to take a course that was a basic introduction to drama after having spent so many months working on stage in theater productions.

I also took a course in stagecraft and another one in stage design and yet another one in stage makeup, all of which focused not on acting, but on how to design and build sets and prepare an actor's face for stage work.

I could hardly wait for the summer of 1958 because I had been accepted to participate as an apprentice actor to perform in the summer theater program at

The Barn Theater in Augusta, Michigan, about 135 miles west of Detroit. The Barn Theater was and still is today a professional Actor's Equity Theater in which amateur apprentices support professionally accredited actors.

Two seasons of participation as an apprentice in the acting program earns the actor an Actor's Equity card that establishes the apprentice as a professional actor and union member able to audition for professional parts on Broadway or anywhere else in the professional theater world.

For those unfamiliar with the term Actor's Equity, it is the United States AFL-CIO-affiliated labor union that represents more than 50,000 actors, actresses, and stage managers. It seeks to advance the careers of its members by negotiating wages and working conditions and by extending a wide range of benefits including health and pension plans. It is similar to the Screen Actors Guild that represents the movie industry and the American Federation of Television and Radio Artists that represents television and radio performers and participants.

As an apprentice actor, I worked in the box office selling theater tickets and worked on shows building sets and generally helping any way I could. I also performed in small parts not being filled by professional actors, such as the paperboy in the play *Picnic* and as part of the chorus in a variety of musicals. In *Guys and Dolls* I was an "extra" and in one scene I had to stand on my hands on a chair as part of a scenario in which two of us apprentices were pretending to be athletes. I was even entrusted with the job of being the stage manager for *Picnic*, since I had previously served as stage manager on several university plays.

The stage manager is a key position in any successful theater production. The position has a unique function because it serves the dual function of assistant to the director and production staff during the rehearsal period, and then becomes the person in charge of the production during the actual performance. It was unusual for an apprentice actor to be given such important responsibilities, but the director knew that I had served as a stage manager in several SIU plays, and he was confident I could successfully carry out the duties and responsibilities on *Picnic*. The play went well without a single hitch, and I received thanks from the professional actors in the cast.

I worked at the Barn Theater all summer, eating there and sleeping there as well. It was a fulfilling and enriching experience that gave me a better insight into professional theater than was possible to get in the university setting. The owner of the theater even paid me a stipend for helping in the box office.

I was assured that if I returned the next year and continued my second year as an apprentice actor I would receive my Actor's Equity card after our third show. Having that card would make it possible for me to audition for professional parts on Broadway in New York City or anywhere else professional actors performed on stage.

One of the professional actors with whom I appeared at the Barn Theater was James Sikking, who in 1981 played the hard-charging and hardheaded SWAT leader Lt. Howard Hunter on the classic television police drama *Hill Street Blues*. He was the lead actor in several of the Barn Theater productions during that summer.

There were other interesting Broadway professional actors at the Barn Theater that summer too, none of whom was acting in Broadway plays at the time. But none of those actors would become as successful or as famous as Sikking. I was delighted to see that Sikking landed such a great part in *Hill Street Blues*. Some years later I ran into him at a friend's house in Brentwood, California just outside of Beverly Hills and we reminisced about our experiences at the Barn Theater. It turned out that Sikking was a friend of my college chum who had worked so many years in Los Angeles as a character actor in the movies.

As I expected, I was invited back to participate for a second year at the Barn Theater in 1959 after which I would receive my Actor's Equity card and become a professional actor, which was my goal throughout my college years; however, during the interim my life changed and I abandoned my ambition to become an actor .

While I was working at The Barn Theater during that summer, Peggy had gone home to be with her family in New England. While she had a sister living in Herrin, Illinois, with whom she lived while she was attending SIU, she was actually from Worcester, Massachusetts, where her mom and dad lived. She spent the summer with them and returned to Herrin to live with her sister just in time for the SIU fall quarter to begin.

Since the city of Herrin is only about 20 miles from Carbondale, it didn't make a lot of sense for Peggy to live with her sister during the school year, because she would have to commute to school every day. So, she and four of her girlfriends rented a house in Carbondale about two miles from campus.

For three months during the fall quarter we dated while she lived with her girlfriends. Then one weekend I took her with me when I went home to visit my mom and family in Alton. My mom loved Peggy right from the start and, of course, everyone in our family knew I was dating her.

While we were in Alton, I took Peggy to meet one of my aunts, a lifelong beautician who worked out of her home. My aunt, who was dad's sister, had always been very close to our family, and I loved to visit with her. She had a son about one year older than me and we had been friends growing up, so I spent a lot of time at their house. His mother, my aunt, had a wonderfully brash personality, and she also loved Peggy from the first moment they met. One day while we were sitting in her beauty parlor she said: "You two are clearly in love. Why don't you get married?" It put me on the spot, but wasn't inappropriate. It was just like her to ask something like that.

I had been thinking about it for quite some time, but had just never gotten around to popping the question. But my aunt's inquiry made us both think about it seriously. It was a bit of an awkward moment because Peggy's sister didn't even want her to date me, let alone marry me. And I knew her sister would throw a fit if we came home and Peggy announced that we were engaged.

Her sister was 12 years older than Peggy and helped raise her. She knew we didn't have much money and figured if we married Peggy would likely quit school and go to work while I finished my degree. And she clearly much preferred for Peggy stay single and complete her education. Besides, I always thought she had visions of Peggy becoming a performer. At any rate she clearly did not favor the idea of us getting married, and I knew we would experience a rough time with her if we even announced an engagement.

Besides, her sister told Peggy that I would never amount to anything. She was confident that marrying me would cause nothing but grief for Peggy. "If you marry him you will never ever know where the next pound of hamburger will come from," she had said.

Nevertheless, we discussed it on the way back to SIU after our visit with mom, and since we were in love, both of us thought it was a great idea, so on January 16, 1959, while I was in my junior year of college, we invited a local justice of the peace over to the house where Peggy was living with her friends, and we got married, despite the disapproval of her older sister.

Her sister was more than a little bit upset about the marriage. In fact, she didn't even speak to me for several years after the marriage, perhaps because just as she had predicted, Peggy quit school and got a job as a nurse's aide at the Carbondale Memorial Hospital. That did not please her sister, and my relationship with her sister was dicey for the rest of her life. For some reason no matter how successful I became, I could not get on her good side. But Peggy healed the wound between her sister and her and they had a very loving relationship. Even now Peggy has nothing but fond and loving memories of her sister. I, not so much!

Peggy worked long hours in a difficult job. She was only 110 pounds but often had to move patients, some of them heavy old men. I really felt bad about her quitting college, but felt reasonably sure she would have other opportunities as we started our marriage and created a new life together.

While I was strong enough to lift Peggy over my head, and frequently did so as a juvenile demonstration of strength, the thought of her lifting sick old men and moving them around the hospital was a bit scary for me. Nevertheless, she continued to work at the hospital until after my graduation. While being a nurse's aide was exhausting and stressed her considerably, she didn't seem to suffer any physical ailments because of it.

We began our marriage by living for a week in a small trailer (8' x 16'), but quickly moved to another trailer that was considerably bigger. After a short period we moved from the trailer into a two-room apartment behind a local movie theater that became available during my senior year. We weren't sure how that would work because of the sometimes-loud movie sounds. Fortunately we were never able to hear anything from the movies.

We had a combined living room and a Pullman kitchen. The kitchen was simply a stove, refrigerator, sink, and cabinet blocked off by a hanging curtain that hid it from the living room. For a short time our kitchen table was an ironing board! We didn't have much furniture, but didn't really need more than a couple of chairs and a couch. I built a bookcase with bricks and 1" x 6" boards and we made do with what little we had. The other room was a combined bedroom and bathroom. The apartment wasn't much but we loved it and lived there until I graduated, after which we lived with her parents for a few weeks until we moved to New Mexico.

The really unusual thing was what happened to her former roommates. Each of them was "going steady" with a college boyfriend while Peggy lived with them, and after graduation each married her boy friend. They didn't all stay married.

Over the years two of them divorced and married someone else. But it was unusual for everyone who had roomed together to marry a "steady boyfriend" so quickly after graduation. We never knew any other group of students to have had a similar experience. We have since lost contact with all but one couple. The single exception lives in northern Illinois, and we hear from them every Christmas.

Meanwhile, during my senior college year, the local Carbondale Air Force recruiter became a casual friend of mine, and to help him with his recruitment goals I agreed to take the Air Force Officer Qualification Test to see if I was eligible for a commission in the Air Force. He sent me to Scott Air Force Base, which is located about 100 miles north of Carbondale and about 20 miles from St. Louis. It's also about 20 miles from my hometown of Alton.

I took and passed the test and was qualified to receive an Air Force commission, but I took the test purely to get recruiting credit for my friend and had no real intention of entering the Air Force. I made him understand that I had no real interest in returning to the military at that time and was only trying to help with his recruiting statistics. So, after my quick trip to Scott Air Force Base to take the test, I went back to my university studies at SIU.

During my junior and senior years I took a lot of theater courses, including courses on Shakespearean tragedies, theater business management, stage make-up, stage lighting, advanced stagecraft, stage management, and advanced acting. All in all I received an excellent preparation for a career in professional theater.

The problem was I had married about nine months before graduation and had to seriously think about our future. Keep in mind that my sister-in-law had already predicted I would not amount to anything. Her husband was an engineer and her two sons became engineers, and one a teacher. From her vantage point there was no way a guy with a theater degree could make a decent living.

What she didn't know was how well my theater experiences and public speaking courses prepared me for work in the public affairs arena in which I would constantly interface with a diverse public. In fact, while I didn't know it at the time, I would eventually occasionally give two or three speeches a week to groups as diverse as high school students and members of local Chambers of Commerce. My theater experiences helped me to feel comfortable in speaking engagements that would scare the pants off most young people. In fact I loved to get up in front of community groups to represent my organizations and did in fact excel at it.

While finishing my senior year at SIU with a new wife to support, I agonized over what to do about my career goals. Getting married put a real wrench in my plans to become a great American actor. I had done lots of research and knew that the odds against success in theater were more than long. The odds were astronomical under the best of conditions and searching for a way to make a reasonable and consistent living in the entertainment world with a new wife didn't inspire me.

It didn't matter whether I was thinking about a stage career on Broadway in New York City or a movie career in Hollywood, my research indicated that except for young people who already had family members who were successful in the business, a form of nepotism, a novice actor could expect months, if not years, waiting for a break that would give him entrance into this difficult and overcrowded field. Literally thousands of young people migrate to Hollywood every year thinking they will overcome the odds against success in that very difficult industry.

I learned that men and women with bachelor and graduate degrees were supporting themselves by waiting on tables in restaurants or working as hotel elevator operators or any one of a number of low-paying jobs to barely make ends meet while waiting for their "big break" in New York and Los Angeles. It is not a cliché to say that young actors can nearly starve to death while waiting for that big break.

It very definitely was not the kind of life I wanted to put my beautiful new wife through, so I discarded all thoughts of a theater or movie career and focused on other ways I could make a living with the skills I had developed while studying theater.

The idea of returning to the military had some appeal for me, especially as a commissioned officer. I had enjoyed my years in the Navy, and remembered the advice I had received from my navy lieutenant supervisor back in 1954. I also remembered that life in the Navy was considerably better for a commissioned officer than it was for an enlisted troop.

After taking the Air Force (AFOQT) test, I had explored Scott Air Force Base and liked what I saw, although I had not seriously considered the Air Force as a career choice.

By then, the Air Force was a glamor branch of the military, largely because we had entered the space age, and the Air Force was getting a lot more attention than the other services. It had other appeals too. I remember while I was in the Navy telling my Army friends, after observing the life my Air Force buddies lived, the beauty of the Air Force was that you get to walk to your bed every night instead of carrying it on your back all day.

The Air Force also had lots of opportunities that could take advantage of my communication skills, especially in the public affairs career field. But I just wasn't ready to commit to a military career, so I considered other possibilities. There wasn't much I could do in the Carbondale area. Other than the university there just weren't many opportunities anywhere in the vicinity of Carbondale. So, I began to think of other possibilities.

CHAPTER 4
A BAD CAREER FIT

As it turned out there was a corporate recruiter working out of an office very near the SIU campus. The recruiter represented the College Life Insurance Company of America, headquartered in Indianapolis, Indiana, which sold life insurance to college students on campuses across America.

While the recruiter, who was also an insurance agent, spent most of his time trying to sell life insurance to students, he also scouted for potential sales recruits who could work for his company. He was absolutely confident that anyone with a theater background would be able to sell life insurance, and he was looking for someone to represent his company in Albuquerque, New Mexico. However, I had no realistic idea of what skills were necessary to sell insurance even though his company appeared to be a legitimate, quality company. Also, I had never considered relocating to that arid-looking state, but I had read about Hollywood celebrities being enamored by Santa Fe and the artist colony in Taos, and I assumed Albuquerque would be equally interesting.

The recruiter was very persuasive that I'd make a good salesman working with college students. After a series of interviews and the prospect of working for a company that had great growth potential and career opportunities for its employees, and his assurances that I'd make a good salesman working with college students, I accepted his offer to represent his company at the University of New Mexico.

Timing was critical. I was anxious about not having a job and not thrilled about continuing to live with my in-laws. I also knew job opportunities were scarce in small-town Carbondale, where there was no industry and perhaps limited positions at the university.

My first task with College Life Insurance Company of America was to train at the company headquarters in Indianapolis where I familiarized myself with the company and its insurance plans.

There were about a dozen new agent-trainees attending the class. The company had previously sent each of us a script, which we had to memorize so we could all work from a unified company presentation. Trainees had to convincingly deliver the presentation in class, in front of other students and faculty members.

Memorizing the sales pitch was not much of a challenge, but not so easy for many of the new agents, especially learning how to deliver the memorized lines with the "illusion of the first time." No salesman wants his pitch to come across as something he has memorized and delivered routinely over the years. For me, it was like learning lines for a play and delivering them with conviction. We studied the company history and how best to respond to insurance questions from prospective customers.

To assist us with sales techniques we sometimes role-played. I found that believing in the product was most helpful and I knew the advantages of buying life insurance at a young age had the benefit of providing the best possible coverage with the lowest-cost premiums. I believed everyone should have a good life insurance policy, especially one to cover funeral expenses.

So off Peggy and I went to begin my new career and discover life in the 'Land of Enchantment' – Albuquerque, New Mexico.

My first experience was not to "enchanting." Just outside Albuquerque my 1956 Ford broke down and I had to postpone our arrival until I got our car fixed. The carburetor failed because it did not have high-altitude jets and couldn't process the correct mixture of gasoline and oxygen. I wasn't expecting a problem from the Albuquerque altitude, but while the city sits at about 5,200 feet, the approach from the Sandia Mountain was more than 6,000 feet, and we had left Alton at an elevation of about 500 feet! High-altitude jets for our carburetor fixed the problem and we continued to the center of Albuquerque.

The look of the city was deceiving. After living in the Midwest much of my life, I had no idea what it would be like to live in what appeared to be a dry, drab looking desert environment. I spent time in San Diego when I was in the navy but this was my first visit to a southwestern state. While it looked dry like Arizona, Albuquerque sits on top of an underground lake, so unlike Arizona it merely looks dry. In fact, the water in the underground lake wasn't drinkable, and until recently the sole source for the city's drinking water was an underground aquifer. But there was plenty of water for sprinkler irrigation. There were patches of green in yards, surrounded by stone sculptured gardens, brown landscapes and typical western adobe architecture.

After about a week in class each of us potential salesmen were well versed in how to answer questions about our company and its products. We had studied and were drilled on prepared responses to potential questions. After an introductory week of practice I felt ready for my new assignment, so I picked up my wife and we drove to Albuquerque.

Our first view of Albuquerque was startling. As we drove over the hill at the entrance to the city we were astonished at the look of Central Avenue, which was the main artery running completely thorough Albuquerque. It was cluttered with garish looking commercial signs advertising companies and products. It just wasn't a sight we had expected and we never got use to that look for the rest of our time in Albuquerque.

But most of our surprise was the general look of the city. I had never seen so many brown or otherwise drab looking houses anywhere I had ever travelled. The Midwest where I had spent most of my life was vibrant and richly colored compared to Albuquerque. We were immediately disappointed in the look of our new city.

Albuquerque sits on U.S. Route 66 between the Sandia Mountain range, which is an absolutely beautiful view on the eastern side of the city, and the Rio Grande River on the western side. The Rio Grande River, which I had read about in high school, was a disappointment. I expected something like the Mississippi or Missouri rivers. Instead the river is so tiny it looked more like a small stream.

Today the Albuquerque population is nearly 600,000, but the population in 1960 was slightly less than half of that. Even so, with a student and faculty population of nearly 30,000 people, logic suggested there would be a fertile population for prospective life insurance sales.

Included in and around Albuquerque were the Sandia National Laboratories, the Petroglyph National Monument, and the Lovelace Respiratory Research Institute. Albuquerque was also known for its Hot Air Balloon Fiesta, which is the largest of its kind in the world and is still very popular today. Other tourist attractions included the Albuquerque Museum of Art and History, its Historic Old Town, the Indian Pueblo Cultural Center, Kirtland Air Force Base, and the New Mexico State Fair, which attracts tourists from multiple state areas and is great for New Mexico businesses.

However, I didn't go to Albuquerque because of its tourist attractions; I went there to sell life insurance to college students. After settling into a small one-bedroom apartment reasonably close to the University, I toured the city to get my bearings, and then I toured the campus to familiarize myself with the layout so I would know where the students hung out. Then I visited the school registrar's office to gather information about the student body and prepared to start work.

I was to discover the most difficult part of the job was getting to meet students and scheduling appointments to discuss the life insurance plans we offered. Even though I had recently graduated from college, I forgot how busy college students could be with classes, homework, extra-curricular activities and their social lives. That meant a lot of evening work for me to fit into their schedules. I also discovered that most students were really not very interested in life insurance. Most of them seemed to think they were immortal and didn't give the possibility of dying a second thought.

It didn't take long to realize the job was not as exciting as I thought it might be. It was challenging, but not exciting. I spent a lot of time on the telephone trying to reach students, and even more time running around the campus trying to reach those I couldn't get on the telephone to coordinate a time and place to meet. It was not easy finding places we could meet where we would not be distracted by interruptions. In their dormitories other students constantly interrupted us, and that made it really difficult to hold the student's attention long enough to pitch our insurance policies.

During a couple of months I amassed an impressive closing rate but not many interviews. When I could make an appointment with a student somewhere that we could be alone for long enough to explain our policies, I did very well. My home office supervisor was excited that I sold insurance polices at about 50 percent of my interviews, but I wasn't able to generate enough interviews to make equally impressive sales statistics. It doesn't do a lot of good to make a sale every other time you pitch the product if you don't have enough sales to cover your salary. I loved working with the students, but trying to sell life insurance to them seemed to be a losing cause.

I soon discovered another issue was money. Most of the students I contacted were not making enough money with their part-time jobs to be able to afford the insurance premiums. Very often mom and dad paid for tuition and books, and provided a stipend to help out with living expenses. That didn't leave much to cover the cost of personal expenses such as life insurance, and young students tended to feel like they didn't really need life insurance anyway. They felt invincible and I never met any of them who thought dying any time soon was even a emote possibility, even though student obits appeared in the local newspaper almost every week.

After about six months I began to suspect that selling life insurance to college students really wasn't in my future. At about the same time the insurance company's leadership came to roughly the same conclusion. They were very gracious, but they had made an investment in me and it wasn't paying off the way they had hoped. So we came to an amicable parting of the ways.

Meanwhile, I liked the concept of life insurance and had received a lot of really good training at College Life Insurance Company of America's Indianapolis office. I also figured a lot of the material I had memorized to sell life insurance and a lot of the experience I had gained since graduating from college would be equally applicable in another sales position at a more familiar insurance company having a much wider potential customer base.

With that in mind I applied for a position with Prudential Insurance Company of America. My family had done business with Prudential for many years and I knew it was a reputable and reliable company. Over the years our Prudential Insurance Company agent stopped by our home in Alton fairly regularly and my family had several life insurance policies with them. Also, since getting married I had taken out a family policy on Peggy and me with Prudential.

With headquarters in Newark, New Jersey and branch offices all over the country, Prudential had over 30,000 employees and was one of the largest and most well respected insurance companies in the United States. I was sure there would be reasonable opportunities with the Prudential Insurance Company.

Over several days I interviewed to become a new Prudential agent, and liked what I heard about the company. It was also clear that they thought I would be an asset to their company. Consequently, I was hired in 1961 to begin my career as a Prudential Insurance debit agent.

I was given a route in Albuquerque for which I was expected to provide whatever insurance support our customers wanted or needed, and to sell new policies to families on my route. Given that Albuquerque had a population of just over quarter million residents at that time, my customer base was immediately improved over the limited number of college students that had previously been my customer base.

For those not familiar with insurance debit routes, a debit agent makes his rounds through a select neighborhood, collecting small insurance premiums in cash and recording the transactions in the homeowner's premium receipt book. Typically the policies were small, as were the premiums. The debit agent was and still is a familiar figure to many Americans. If you owned this kind of insurance and lived on a Prudential route it was not unusual for you to see your agent every week or two.

The official name for these weekly policies was "Industrial" insurance policies, and while many people could not come up with enough money to pay a large annual premium for a policy large enough to provide a legacy amount for their family, they were able to raise small amounts to cover a weekly or monthly premium for a smaller policy. And since the Prudential agent often met with his customers every week or two he had lots of opportunity to review the insurance needs of an entire family.

As I began to work the route assigned to me, which covered a fairly sizeable area of the northern part of Albuquerque, I noticed that lots of families had relatively large insurance policies on the breadwinner, usually a husband or father, to protect the family in case the head of the family died unexpectedly. But often other family members had little or no coverage. And, if they had any insurance coverage for mom and the kids it was usually small amounts of coverage. I was never able to understand the logic in that since we all eventually need a minimum amount of insurance to cover the costs of medical bills that often followed the death of an individual and the eventual cost of burials. And since we are all going to die it made sense to me that every member of a family should at least have enough insurance coverage to cover the burial expenses.

In the 1960s cremation was a fairly uncommon choice; most people were buried in a cemetery, so a body needed to be prepared for a viewing in a coffin and a place to hold a wake, all of which generally costs more than cremation. It could put quite a dent into a family's finances if a proper amount of life insurance wasn't available to cover the costs.

Having an established debit route of collections gave me an opportunity to become friends with the families, and most of them were glad to see me whenever I came by their home. In fact it was not uncommon to be offered a cup of coffee when I stopped by to collect their premiums and sometimes the visits were as much social as business.

I got to know a lot of my customers personally and began to talk to them about the wisdom of having small policies on each family member—just a few thousand dollars—enough to cover burial expenses in case someone in the family died unexpectedly. That worked well and generated an appreciable uptick in my insurance sales, but more importantly it provided emergency coverage for my customers.

I next made an appointment with many of the family breadwinners to discuss the wisdom of having a small industrial policy, $500-1,000, on the breadwinner's life just to cover expenses until the larger policies were paid out when the head of the family died. That amount of money went a lot further in 1962 than it does today.

Since an individual's income stream might stop completely as soon as death occurs, the family would need a source of income to carry them over until the larger settlement arrived. I found that a lot of my customers thought that was a great idea, especially because the premiums for those small policies tended to be really small amounts.

As you might expect over a period of a few months I sold a lot of small policies in the $500-1,000 range. Needless to say that went over well with my Prudential supervisor, and we scheduled a time when I could meet with the entire branch of insurance agents and brief them about my sales approach. During that briefing I explained my sales philosophy and emphasized the need to offer a way for families to sustain themselves during a death crisis.

My presentation went over well and there was an almost immediate uptick in our office sales of small industrial policies for the head of household, plus sales of small policies to family members other than the breadwinner. I no longer remember what the long-term benefits of those experiences were for the company, but I remember that my supervisor was pleased.

I continued to meet regularly with folks who lived on my debit route and even when I went short periods without any sales I still enjoyed the time I spent with them.

However, I had a problem. Even though I was excited to be able to help my customers with their insurance needs, many of who became my friends, overall the work bored me. I just didn't feel like selling insurance policies for the long term was something I wanted to do with my life. I had no problem with the value of my work, which I knew would eventually benefit my customers, but it didn't really excite me and I just didn't see me doing it for the next 30-40 years. I knew a lot of agents who had spent their entire adult lives as insurance agents, but I couldn't see that in my future. I spent a lot of time thinking about whether it was time once again to change the direction of my career.

I struggled with the internal conflict this dilemma caused me for several more months, but finally decided selling life insurance just wasn't going to satisfy me long term. I just didn't see me as a salesman, even though I knew I had some talent in that arena. Not just insurance. I didn't want to sell anything. While I had an excellent closing rate on my sales, I didn't enjoy trying to persuade people who weren't interested and sometimes couldn't afford to buy what I was selling.

I knew people who were happy selling clothes in the local mall, and others who sold real estate or cars, or any number of other tangible items, but sales just wasn't something I wanted to do. So, once more I decided I needed a change. I had a good run as a Prudential debit agent, but I wasn't satisfied with my career. So, I thanked my Prudential supervisor for the opportunities the company had given me, and I thanked my fellow agents for their support. I apologized to my customers and I stopped selling insurance.

I wasn't prepared for the reaction I got from the customers on my route. Many were disappointed that I would no longer be representing them. I had not really thought of how they might look at it. I had become friendly with many of them and some didn't think of me as representing Prudential; they thought of me as their personal insurance representative. That gave me really mixed emotions. While I was sure selling insurance was not a good fit for me, I was gratified that so many of my customers trusted me and felt comfortable having me look after their insurance interests. While I was confident in my decision to give up insurance as a career path, I left with a heavy heart because of the affection I felt for so many of my customers.

While selling life insurance I noticed another company that we often interfaced with, particularly when selling policies that were substantially larger than normal. We used a company called Retail Credit Company to investigate potential customers when we suspected there might be an ulterior motive for suddenly purchasing a new large insurance policy. It was not uncommon for people who suffered from potentially fatal health issues to try to get a large life insurance policy approved so they could leave a financial legacy for their families.

The name Retail Credit Company was somewhat of a misnomer. It did not extend credit to people. It was an investigative firm that did personal and personnel investigations to determine if individuals were an unnecessary or unusual risk for corporations and companies, such as insurance companies.

Prudential knew that it could be the source of financial compensation for families when a loved one died. That was expected when death occurred naturally at the end of life expectancy, but it also knew it had to protect itself from risks associated with customers who waited until a medical prognosis of imminent death before deciding to increase their insurance coverage so they could leave a financial legacy at the expense of Prudential . It was Prudential's job to determine whether a potential customer was an unusual risk, and they used the Retail Credit Company to assess that risk.

Knowing that Retail Credit Company did investigations for our particular branch of the Prudential Insurance Company, I requested and was granted an interview for a potential job as a Retail Credit Company investigator. Much to my surprise, after a lengthy interview with the local supervisor, because of my insurance background the supervisor thought I would make a good investigative agent for their company. So, he hired me on a temporary basis and assigned me to another agent to shadow for a week. That meant I would accompany him on his investigations for a week and observe how he approached individuals to gather personal information about individuals we thought might be a security risk to a life insurance company.

It looked like something I might be good at. It involved interviewing people who knew the insurance applicant, such as neighbors or co-workers, to determine if they knew anything that might raise a red flag making the potential customer a serious risk. The work was mostly outside and involved a lot of walking, which I liked. Even more importantly with that kind of work I knew no two days would ever be the same, or so I thought. Little did I realize at that point how very much we are all alike. We tend to think of ourselves as separate and distinctly different individuals, with distinctly different personalities. But we really have much in common.

I shadowed another agent during my first week on the job and watched him interview people. It didn't seem to be very difficult until I began to realize how analytical the job really was. The interviewer really doesn't have to say much. Once he establishes the nature of the interview it becomes more of a listening issue than a talking issue.

We would explain that we were there to see how his neighbors viewed our applicant and to learn if they thought there was any reason he or she might have any problems about which the insurance company ought to know.

After the opening remarks we would form our next questions based on what the neighbor had to say in answer to the previous one. For instance, the conversation might go like this:

Me: How well do your neighbors seem to get along?

Neighbor: They get along wonderfully well since the baby came! They are absolutely great neighbors now.

Me: How well did they get along before the baby came?

Neighbor: They were very quiet before the baby came. Since the baby they have become really friendly and everybody seems to like them now.

Me. Do you know if they quarrel much?

Neighbor: They don't seem to argue any more since the baby came.

Me. Do you know if the husband or wife is a hunter?

Neighbor: I think he hunts from time to time but I can't be sure.

That led me into a discussion about how the people I interviewed and the insurance applicant felt about guns, which are often used to commit suicide. There are a whole series of questions that can be asked about how guns are stored and used.

Incidentally that is an actual conversation I had with a particular neighbor in Albuquerque. Each question leads you to your next question until you feel as though you have learned something important about the insurance applicant, particularly as it relates to the applicant being a risk for the insurance company. Some people might think the job was to gather gossip; it was not. The job was to assess risk to a company as accurately as possible.

Just as important is whether or not additional interviews with other neighbors can confirm the information gleaned from the first interview. If two or three neighbors all seemed to confirm the same information it strengthened the agent's recommendation to the company about the advisability of issuing a new insurance policy to the applicant.

After the first week shadowing an agent I was sent out into the field to conduct my own interviews. I investigated people all over Albuquerque, and I was absolutely shocked at how much information neighbors will voluntarily share about each other. In the previous conversation, the housewife who told me how well her neighbors got along since the baby was born had no idea how comments like that lead to questions about how and why they didn't get along before the baby was born, which goes to the state of mind of her neighbors and can lead to more in-depth questions about their history.

Once the interviews are completed in that neighborhood, the agent must get back in his car and make explicit notes so he will be prepared to make a detailed report when he returns to his office. Notes had to be detailed and complete because the agents could one day be required to testify for the company in open court, and his notes must support the report he files with the company. These reports are confidential and the insurance applicant can never know the content even if the insurance he wants is denied to him. Most of the time the insurance applicant doesn't even know the insurance company is checking on him or her. And, as far as I knew denial of insurance was a fairly rare occurrence.

During my time with the Retail Credit Company I never heard of anyone actually being subpoenaed to appear in court, but preparation was essential just in case. And, even if there was no possibly of a court case the agent must be prepared to defend his company report to his supervisor.

I continued to do background investigations for insurance companies, while other agents did personnel selection background checks on prospective new employees for companies and corporations. After a few months doing investigations all over Albuquerque, I was sent to do the same thing in Grants and Gallup, New Mexico. Grants, with a population of almost 9,000, is about 80 miles directly west from Albuquerque; Gallup, with a population of almost 22,000 is about 140 miles west from Albuquerque.

There wasn't enough investigative business in either Grants or Gallup to warrant a full-time agent stationed there, so I would go over and conduct our business there for three or four days and come back to Albuquerque long enough to write-up my company reports and stay home for the weekend.

There was a large Native American population in the Gallup area, particularly Navajo Indians, so I frequently had to investigate Indians. I found the best source of reliable information about local Indians was people who worked in the downtown area, e.g., merchants and small shopkeepers. The Indians came to town frequently during the week, particularly after payday, and seemed to be well known wherever they shopped. Civic leaders and most of the local population I met were very proud of their Navajo Indians and I never had any trouble checking on those who came to town regularly. But I had some unusual and interesting cases among the general population.

I remember one time I was investigating a single mother in Grants who had let her insurance policy lapse because she couldn't afford to make the premiums, but suddenly wanted to renew her policy. Our company was suspicious that there was some unique reason she suddenly wanted to renew a policy she had recently cancelled. It was unusual for a policyholder to let a policy lapse and then after a brief time try to renew it. It suggested an important change in the life of the policyholder.

I questioned neighbors for quite awhile because they seemed reluctant to talk about her. That was really unusual because most of the time neighbors in Grants were very friendly. I sensed there was something amiss. She had two young children and seemed to be quite protective of them. I don't remember whether she was divorced or widowed, but she was taking care of the children by herself.

She was very reluctant to answer my questions directly, particularly when I asked about her recent health. She really avoided answering health related issues. Once I gently but firmly made it clear that I would continue checking until I was comfortable there was nothing afoot in her life, particularly in her recent past since letting her policy lapse, she gave up what had been a charade.

She was wearing a scarf around her neck and finally said OK as she removed the scarf to reveal a large scar that covered both sides of her neck. She had recently tried to commit suicide by slashing her throat. She had missed her jugular or would have bled out. Meanwhile she was trying to get her insurance policy reinstated so she could leave money to her children if or when she tried it again.

It was a terribly sad scene. She was so disappointed that she had been found out but she should have known she couldn't pass muster with such a huge scar on her throat. I felt sorry for her but there was nothing I could do; I had no choice but to report my findings to our company and based on our report the insurance company quickly denied her request to reinstate her insurance policy. I never knew whatever happened to her after that. I never ran into her anywhere in town and nobody ever mentioned her to me again.

While the work was certainly interesting, there were just too many cases that left me feeling like I was helping my company but hurting the people I was investigating. Cases like that were so depressing to me that I began to think once more about whether or not I should reconsider my decision to not re-enter the military. It wasn't just that I wasn't happy with my work, although that was a major part of it.

In the two years I lived in Albuquerque I really didn't care for it much, and I really didn't care for working in Grants and Gallup. While it was wonderful to go up into the Sandia Mountains on a weekend and have a great cookout, I never ever got used to the drab colors and dry look. The annual state fair was extraordinary but that wasn't enough to keep us in New Mexico. I missed the green look that covered the Midwest. My wife shared my feelings about New Mexico.

She had a good job working for the local power and electric company, but she too was not thrilled about staying in Albuquerque for the long term. Neither of us liked the desert look and all the drab colored houses and commercial buildings. The residents and local merchants were friendly, but we just were not happy with the city. We had made some really wonderful friends, but of all the places we had lived Albuquerque was our least favorite, so I talked to her about the possibility of me returning to the military. I was pretty sure I didn't want to return to the Navy and I wasn't interested in the Army, so from my perspective that only left the Air Force. The Coast Guard wasn't even an option.

I was perceptive enough to know that part of my being unhappy with Albuquerque was my inability to find a good career fit. I knew I had always enjoyed my time in the navy, and suspected I would probably enjoy a full military career. Since I had already passed the Air Force Officer Qualification Test (AFOQT) I knew it would not be difficult to get a commission. While I liked my time in the Navy when I was single, especially because of the wonderful travel, I didn't think it was a good fit for my marriage. Also, I didn't look forward to spending 12 or 14 years at sea and I knew about the high divorce rate among navy couples.

With that in mind, I knew I didn't want to make a career in the Navy. So I visited with the local Air Force recruiter who assured me since I already earned a college degree, I could go through the nine and one-half-week Air Force Officer Training School (OTS) program at Lackland Air Force Base in San Antonio, Texas, after which I would be commissioned a Second Lieutenant. He suggested there was also a very good chance I could be assigned to the major command of my choice and be assigned somewhere in mid-America.

I took some time to think about it and discussed the possibility with my Retail

Credit Company supervisor. I made no pretense about making a career with Retail Credit Company, but they had been good to me and I wanted to be straight with them. My supervisor had previously served in the Air Force and tried to discourage me by claiming the best I could hope for would be a reserve officer corps commission that would not guarantee me an Air Force career. He thought I had a better career opportunity with Retail Credit Company.

It was his opinion that with a reserve commission I would have a hard time trying to make it to the 20-year retirement point. He didn't know many Air Force reserve officers who were offered a regular commission, which is the best insurance an individual can have to make it through to retirement. He acknowledged there was always a chance I would get a regular commission but he didn't think the odds were very good.

I knew, however, that I would have a jump on a military career because I had already served eight years in the Navy (a combination of active duty and inactive reserve status). While the inactive reserve period would not count toward retirement it would count for longevity pay. That meant I would start off with a little bit more money than the average Second Lieutenant and a modest jump on retirement.

My supervisor at the Retail Credit Company seemed to be genuinely disappointed that I was thinking of leaving the company to join the Air Force. He liked the way I did my investigations and wrote up my reports. In fact he all but assured me of a promotion if I stayed with the company, but that didn't have very much appeal to me.

After thinking back over the nearly two years of working in insurance and investigations I knew that my future would probably not be in Albuquerque, or in the insurance or investigative businesses. I didn't want to start looking for yet another change in my civilian career path, so I contacted the Air Force recruiter, discussed my career path options, especially to what field I could expect to be assigned, filled out the paperwork and joined the Air Force. Peggy agreed that seemed like my best move.

During the early stages of my discussions with the Air Force recruiter I explained that I had a Bachelor of Science degree in communications, with emphasis in theater and speech courses, and lots of experience working with customers. While the recruiter was quick to assure me I would be selected to attend Air Force Officer Training School, after which I would be commissioned a

Second Lieutenant, I made it clear I would only join the Air Force if I could be assigned to a career field that was compatible with and took advantage of my communications background. He assured me that I would be selected to enter the Information Services career field, which was a euphemism for its public affairs career field.

Over the years the Department of Defense had decided the military did not need public relations professionals, so it eliminated that career field. However, the Air Force knew otherwise, so it simply changed the name of the career path to the misnomer: Information Services. Later, during the early years of my Air Force career the Department of Defense recognized it had made a mistake and created a public relations department of its own, which is the Office of the Assistant Secretary of Defense for Public Affairs (OASD/PA).

The formal explanation for the OASD/PA was and still is: The ASD/PA (public affairs) is the principal staff advisor and assistant to the Secretary of Defense and Deputy Secretary of Defense for public information, internal information, community relations, information training, and audiovisual matters. Call it what you like but it is a public relations department.

With that in mind, the Air Force brought the function back out of the closet and renamed it the public affairs career field, which is the field to which the recruiter assured me I would be assigned and the field in which I spent my entire Air Force career.

Bravo! After nearly two years working as an insurance agent and investigator, I was finally assured that I would be able to have a career in a communications field for which my educational training and work experience had prepared me. I was extremely excited to return to the military, apprehensive but excited.

It's possible the reader will not immediately see the correlation between my university studies in theater, especially with so much focus on acting, but the combination of my theater education, training and experience and the many public speaking courses I took in college, combined with my customer relations experience with the insurance and investigative fields prepared me well to serve as an interface between an organization such as the Air Force and the general public. I was better prepared than the typical new college graduate to handle the nuances of stage fright than most people feel when they are committed to speak publicly.

I felt I was better prepared for this new adventure than any I had addressed thus far in my relatively young life, and I looked forward to my new challenges with great excitement. I was going to be a brand new commissioned officer in the U.S. Air Force. That meant I had to straighten up my affairs in Albuquerque and arrange for Peggy to go stay with her mom and dad while I was attending OTS. Our next step together would be an assignment to a new base somewhere in the United States.

CHAPTER 5
A CAREER IN THE AIR FORCE

The U.S. Air Force sent me to Lackland Air Force Base in San Antonio, Texas to attend its Officer Training School (OTS) program. The Air Force initiated OTS at Medina Annex, Lackland AFB in 1959. The school subsequently moved to Maxwell AFB in September 1993 as part of the Air Force chief of staff's vision to align all officer education and training under its Air University.

According to Colonel Stephen P Frank, Commandant of the OTS program,

"...the primary mission at OTS is to produce leaders of moral character in an environment of mutual respect and dignity. To do that the school has highly motivated and exceptionally talented instructors who are dedicated to making sure that every student who passes thorough OTS develops skills necessary to becoming an outstandingly successful Air Force officer."

. . .

While that sounds like hyperbole, I can vouch for the fact that it is actually true. The program was a rigorous nine and one-half weeks of courses that covered a variety of subjects taught in classrooms, such as Leadership, The Profession of Arms, Communications, and Warfare Studies. Of course, an equally rigorous physical training program taught outside on the tarmac and athletic fields accompanied the classroom study.

Like my naval boot camp training, the OTS course included several team sports, including softball, volleyball and flickerball. Flickerball would make a great competitive college sport and could potentially earn some favor as a professional sport.

I quickly learned that OTS was very much like the boot camp experiences I endured in the Navy, only all the classes and training were slanted toward the need for students to learn techniques of leadership and teamwork to prepare them to become Air Force officers. The primary focus for everything we learned was on the importance of functioning as a cohesive unit, whether in the classroom or on the field.

I also reminded myself, as I had in naval boot camp, that the course could not stop time. No matter how difficult the chores, and some of the training was tough, at the end of nine and one-half weeks we would graduate and become second lieutenants.

OTS was divided into four segments: indoctrination, development, application, and transition. The first phase was designed to teach students the basics of leadership and military management. The second phase focused on developing an understanding of leadership and the Air Force culture. During the third phase students are put through exercises that gave them an opportunity to demonstrate how well they understood hands-on leadership. And the fourth phase helped them transition from the training environment into the operational Air Force. It's where all the classroom courses and physical training culminated in graduation and the students receipt of their first assignment into the "real" Air Force.

As had been true in naval boot camp, some of the OTS students didn't complete the course. I'll leave it to your imagination to appreciate why some of them just could not excel at the physically demanding part of training. Some college kids simply had made it through college without anyone ever demanding that they shape up physically or mentally. Many had never had a job because mom and dad supported them from birth to graduation from college.

OTS courses were more challenging than typical college students experience either at home or in school. For some it was an exciting challenge they enjoyed; for others it was more intimidating than anything they had expected. For me it was simply something I anticipated, looked forward to, and knew would culminate in a way to begin my Air Force career.

ADC/NORAD, Truax Field, Madison, Wisconsin.

No matter our backgrounds, initially we were all excited to get our new assignments. My first assignment was, as the recruiter had promised, to the public affairs office of an Air Defense Command (ADC)/North American Aerospace

Defense Command (NORAD) division at Truax Field, in Madison, Wisconsin. Today it is Truax Field Air National Guard Base.

Peggy had gone home to visit her parents while I completed OTS, so the first thing I did after receiving my "brown bars" as a second lieutenant was to go visit with her family for a few days, after which we drove to Madison where my Air Force career began. Incidentally, unlike her sister, her mom and dad treated me with great kindness and affection.

It was an exciting time for me. NORAD is a bi-national United States and Canadian organization charged with the missions of aerospace warning and aerospace control for North America. Aerospace warning includes the monitoring of man-made objects in space, and the detection, validation, and warning of attacks against North America whether by aircraft, missiles, or space vehicles, through mutual support arrangements with other commands. Aerospace control includes ensuring air sovereignty and air defense of the airspace of Canada and the United States. That is a fancy way of saying our mission was to protect the United States and Canada from any outside threats to our countries.

As a joint command, Canadians as well as Americans were assigned to our unit, and my first boss in the Air Force was a Canadian flight lieutenant, the equivalent of an American Air Force captain. He was an excellent boss professionally and was socially gregarious. My wife and I developed a social relationship with he and wife, despite our rank differences. Unfortunately his Achilles heel was his penchant for alcohol.

Years later, on a visit to Canada I found an entirely different person. He had refrained from alcohol, was completely sober, and even warned me of the dangers of drinking. At dinner that night, with his new wife, he got quite upset when his wife and I ordered wine. It has been about twenty-five years since that visit and I pray my friend has maintained his sobriety.

Even though I was only a second lieutenant we were close in age because of my previous naval experience. It was amusing walking around base because while most second lieutenants wore one or maybe two service ribbons on their chest, I had three rows of ribbons from my prior service. It shocked people, and I got a lot of stares because most of them couldn't figure out how a "brown bar" could have so many ribbons. I always got a kick out of watching the strange looks. It was as if nobody had ever seen a second lieutenant with so much brass on his chest, which was probably true, although it should have been an immediate indication that I had risen through the ranks and was not new to the military.

While I spent some of my time working with the local news media answering questions related to NORAD, I also spent time escorting local celebrities and news media representatives on tours of NORAD headquarters in Colorado Springs, Colorado. That was always exciting because NORAD headquarters is located deep in the heart of the Cheyenne Mountain Range and I was always as impressed with it, as were our guests.

While assigned to ADC/NORAD I took an Air University course on the Air Force information services (public affairs) career field. While it was informational and instructional, I learned more from my Canadian flight lieutenant boss and non-commissioned officers assigned to our office.

One of the more interesting aspects of my assignment to NORAD at Truax Field was our public participation in radio broadcasts of NORAD's tracking of Santa Claus. For a couple of weeks I would broadcast on a local radio station, several times each day, our progress of tracking Santa Claus as he approached the United States from the North Pole. Evidently the Air Force is still tracking Santa over the Christmas period because I heard several of their reports on a radio station in Florida in 2017.

My tenure with NORAD at Truax Field didn't last long, less than a year, because my mother-in-law was diagnosed with metastatic cancer and was not expected to live for long. For health reasons my in-laws moved from Massachusetts to Connecticut to live with Peggy's sister and brother-in-law. My father-in-law also had serious heart issues, so it was a difficult time for the family.

I requested a humanitarian assignment to a base closer to Connecticut so Peggy would be able to visit her parents on weekends. The Air Force granted my request and assigned me to the 4603rd Air Base Group at Stewart Air Force Base, New York, on the outskirts of Newburgh, about 60 miles north of New York City. Stewart AFB was home to a B-57 squadron.

By then Peggy's mom had moved in with Peggy's sister who was living in Plainville, Connecticut, which was about 120 miles from Stewart AFB, almost a straight-line drive east on U.S. Interstate 84. Once we were settled in our off-base house at Stewart we drove to Connecticut every weekend that I was able to get away from my Air Force duties. I became very familiar with U.S. Interstate 84 that crosses New York and Connecticut, and we continued visiting her sister in Connecticut as often as possible during my tour of duty at Stewart Air Force Base.

Stewart Air Force Base, Newburgh, New York

After a few months at Stewart AFB, the base commander decided it would be a lot more efficient and convenient for me to be available on base around the clock, so he jumped me to the head of the waiting list for on-base housing. As it turned out that was a prescient move because I would become involved in issues that required my fairly constant presence on base.

Stewart was part of the Air Defense Command (ADC) and NORAD, and there was a NORAD division headquarters stationed on base as a tenant unit. However, I had nothing to do with that unit. I was assigned to Stewart as the base public affairs officer, responsible for public affairs for the entire base.

Part of my responsibilities included providing public affairs support for the 4713th Defense Systems Evaluation Squadron that flew B-57 Canberra aircraft out of Stewart AFB. The Martin B-57 Canberra is an American-built, twinjet tactical bomber and reconnaissance aircraft that entered service with the United States Air Force in 1953. The B-57 is a license-built version of the British English Electric Canberra, manufactured by the Glenn L. Martin Company. Initial Martin-built models were highly similar to their British-built counterparts. Martin later modified the design to incorporate larger quantities of US-sourced components and produced the aircraft in several variants. According to its manufacturer the B-57 Canberra holds the distinction of being the first jet bomber in United States service to drop bombs during extensive combat in South Vietnam.

The B-57 had a crew of two, a pilot and a navigator. Its function flying out of Stewart was to provide Electronic Counter-Measure (ECM) training and evaluation services to various aircraft control and warning squadrons at other bases. Its crew tried to penetrate American and Canadian air defenses to identify any weakness in our Air Defense Command/NORAD system.

The Martin B-57 Canberra, originally developed as a medium bomber for Tactical Air Command, was being phased out in favor of the F-100 Super Sabre. Some of these B-57s were reassigned from Griffiss AFB in Rome, New York to Stewart AFB, when Griffiss AFB was turned over to the Strategic Air Command.

Early in my tenure at Stewart AFB I was promoted to first lieutenant and became friends with quite a few B-57 pilots and navigators and eventually had to field news media inquiries regarding B-57 crashes involving pilots with whom I was more than a little bit familiar. It was always difficult to respond to news media inquiries about B-57 crashes when they involved a pilot or navigator with whom I was reasonably close. One time I had to deal with media inquiries about a crash that involved a crew I had been drinking with at the Officer's Club only a few evenings before the incident.

As an aside, the B-57 was used extensively in South Vietnam. According to the book, *B-57 Canberra Units of the Vietnam War*:

"while not receiving as much publicity as the F-105 and F-4 fighter-bombers, which took the fight into the heart of North Vietnam, the B-57 Canberra was nevertheless the first jet-powered American attack aircraft committed to the conflict. It was involved in day-to-day interdiction missions against traffic coming down the Ho Chi Minh Trail, shooting up trucks and bombing and strafing sampans in the Mekong Delta. And, not least of all, the aircraft flew classified 'black' missions over the border into Laos and Cambodia."

Initially in 1964 they served at our base in Bien Hoa, but later served at other bases too.

While stationed at Steward AFB a staff of four enlisted men and a secretary were assigned to me to help with whatever public affairs support was necessary. In addition to our regular duties we also published a weekly base newspaper titled the *Stewart Guardian*, which featured weekly coverage of happenings around the base and our major air command.

Our newspaper covered anything that involved our B-57s and general information that would be of interest to military residents. In addition to internal information, anything negative that happened off base that required public affairs support was also my responsibility. For instance, over a six-month period I was responsible for all news media coverage associated with three major off-base B-57 accidents, which meant I was also responsible for all public affairs issues associated with those accidents.

To do my job I had to gather as much factual information as I could gather as quickly as possible so I would be prepared for national, regional, and local news media inquiries. That meant being one of the first on-scene base representatives to visit the crash site, so I could gather factual information and be the focal point and source of information for reporters who would often be some of the first responders at the crash site.

At the same time I had to make sure my answers to public and internal inquiries were couched in terms that wouldn't further devastate our flight crew's family members. That was particularly important when one of our aircraft went down at sea because of the raw emotions of the crew's family members.

I was also responsible for issues of concern to my higher headquarters, which was particularly important whenever we were dealing with a crisis.

While we had to answer inquiries factually, I always wanted to make sure the family members of the crew were assured we would never quit looking for their husband or other relatives. We did not want them to read in a news report or hear on the radio or on television that we had said their next of kin was lost at sea and presumed to be dead. That sometimes called for some delicate phraseology to be both factual yet reassuring to the family.

Another area that required extensive public affairs focus was on our yearly Armed Forces Day "open house," in which we opened the base to the general public to view static displays of aircraft and to attend briefings on our missions and roles. While the base operations office was responsible for setting up displays on our flight line, my responsibility was to handle all news media relations for the event, which typically ran for a weekend. We also held an annual Armed Forces Day program, which was much like the Armed Forces Day "open house." While they were similar, they were not the same. One was an open house where visitors could learn a lot about our base. The other was mostly a static display they could visit on the flight line.

The first Armed Forces Day program I promoted generated an attendance of just over 42,000 people from Newburgh and surrounding communities. Our flight line was full of visitors learning about our aircraft and flight line equipment. Our Armed Forces Day Open House was always a lot of fun for local citizens, especially the kids who liked to climb all over our aircraft. Not literally, but we always had a ramp available so they could climb up and look into the cockpit.

Next came the Kiwanis Kids Day program that attracted more than 1,000 local participants (children) in support of the national program. Mostly we brought kids on base and put on a fancy information program at the base theater. Of course the base theater could not hold 1,000 kids at one time so we divided them into two groups and staggered their briefings, entertaining one group with displays while the other group was being briefed in the movie theater.

In each instance I worked with the local newspaper and regional TV outlets to let the public know about these programs and their opportunity to visit our base during the Armed Forces Day open house. I also spoke to local civic groups, inviting them to tell their members about our open house.

Invariably we had a huge turnout from the local communities and received a lot of positive news media coverage. The relations we established with the community and the understanding it generated was particularly helpful when it was necessary to garner community support for our missions, especially during periods when we had citizen complaints about noise from aircraft flying over their neighborhoods. We took noise abatement steps for our aircraft to fly evasive patterns, particularly on takeoffs to minimize noise, but there was no way to avoid the noise completely.

I was and still am mystified by complaints from people who live directly under the flight path of commercial and military aircraft when the Air Force bases and airports existed long before contractors built and sold houses there. It has always seemed unrealistic to me for new homeowners in those areas to believe the bases and airports should move now that citizens live in their flight path. Nevertheless, citizens tended to complain about aircraft noises, and I still had to serve as the focal point for citizen noise complaints.

Another interesting area for which I was responsible was handling UFO inquiries. We had a local citizen who advertised himself as a tri-county focal point for all UFO reports. What that meant was that anyone who saw anything he or she didn't understand or couldn't identify as an airplane would report the sighting to him, and he would report it to me. I would then notify our base operations people, and they would identify someone our base commander could appoint as an investigator to check out the report. In all the time I was at Stewart AFB nothing serious ever developed from a UFO sighting. In essence the UFO sightings were something between a curiosity and a nuisance. But we paid serious attention to them and local citizens appreciated our efforts to make sure the sightings didn't pose any kind of a threat to their communities.

From day to day my responsibilities were fairly routine. They mostly required that I manage my team efficiently, with tact and concern for the morale of our department and the welfare of our base. It was also important for us to have good community relations, and I often spoke to local civic groups about our base missions, personnel, and equipment. I made sure they understood that we took every precaution to minimize noise when we flew over their homes.

During 1964 Peggy and I decided to take a vacation from the daily pressures and lay on the beach at a hotel on Miami Beach. It was actually our first honeymoon. I no longer remember which hotel we stayed in but we had an enjoyable time. The most memorable part of the vacation didn't happen on the beach; it happened at the Miami International Airport.

While waiting for a flight home, my wife had to use the bathroom, so she scouted around until she found a woman's restroom and entered a stall. When she turned to place a cover on the seat, she noticed something very shiny in the already flushed toilet. The water was clean and when she looked closer she saw what looked like gold jewelry, so she used a souvenir swizzle stick from her purse to retrieve it, and discovered it was an expensive looking Omega watch attached to a spectacular gold and jewel encrusted bracelet. Obviously an heirloom!

Clearly some woman had accidentally dropped it or caught it on her clothing while completing her use of the toilet, and obviously didn't notice that it was missing. In the middle of the Miami International airport there was no way to find its owner, so she ran water over it and we took it home. Peggy took the piece to a neighborhood jeweler who said he couldn't accurately appraise it because some stones were chipped or missing, but it was clearly an expensive heirloom watch and bracelet, that had special meaning for whoever had it created.

We advertised in the "lost and found" section of the Miami newspapers but nobody responded to them, so we kept the watch for many years. Even though we know the original owner perhaps paid thousands of dollars for the watch, Peggy eventually sold it to a jeweler for $600. But, to this day the image of her fishing the watch out of the toilet is enough to bring a smile to my face (she claims it was a clean extraction, sanitized under a facuet!)

Meanwhile, I continued to serve as the base public affairs officer, and the Air Force sent me to Boston University to take a two-month short course in public information, which included graduate courses in public relations, mass communications, advertising and marketing for which the university gave me 10 credit hours of graduate school credit toward a Master of Science degree.

It was an excellent program managed especially for Air Force public affairs officers. It was also profitable for the university since the Air Force sent about two-dozen officers to attend each class. The courses formed an excellent background that prepared officers, especially junior officers who had not worked in the public affairs career field for very long, with the fundamentals necessary to represent the Air Force well in the public affairs career field.

Unfortunately, during the 1960s, while the United States was fighting a war in South Vietnam, there was huge unrest on campus, with students demonstrating daily against America's participation in the war generally and the university's support of our Air Force public affairs program specifically. To minimize our presence on campus, we Air Force students wore civilian clothes, grew our hair and sideburns longer than usual, and generally tried to blend in by avoiding calling attention to our presence on campus. Even so, because of our age and dress differences, we stuck out like a sore thumbs.

There was one incident I remember particularly well. During a rather nasty student protest, several students pulled the American flag down from its pole and took it off of its lanyard. A former Air Force veteran (not one of our public affairs students) saw them do it. He rushed over to the two students and ripped the flag out of their hands, put it back on the lanyard and raised it to where it was supposed to be. He then turned to the two students and said as I recall, "if you want that flag you're going to have to come through me to get it." He was a fairly sizeable fellow who looked like he was prepared to deal with the two students in a way they hadn't expected. After that the students moved on to protest somewhere else on campus.

For months students put so much pressure on the university that it withdrew from the Air Force program completely, forcing the Air Force to close down its on-campus program. To continue its educational program for new public affairs officers the Air Force established a similar program on campus at the University of Oklahoma, which continues today.

Once the United States withdrew from the war in South Vietnam, student demonstrations at Boston University ceased and the university invited the Air Force to return with its pubic affairs program. By then the Air Force was pleased with the University of Oklahoma program and declined Boston University's offer. I never heard what Boston University's reaction was to the Air Force decision, but I know it cost Boston University a lot of money to cater to these immature, unruly, and unpatriotic students. While I never said anything to anybody at the university, I was not impressed with the university's shortsighted leadership who kicked the Air Force off campus to cater to an unruly group of noisy students.

Meanwhile, I returned to Stewart AFB where I continued to run the base pubic affairs program, including an internal program that focused on keeping base personnel informed about base-wide, major command, and Air Force programs, and a community relations program in which I was the base interface with the local community.

A little known benefit of being assigned to Stewart was its location, approximately 17 miles from West Point, the U.S. Army's military academy. West Point and Stewart had jointly financed a magnificent 18-hole golf course at West Point, and because Stewart was a joint sponsor of the golf course anyone assigned to our base was entitled to play on the West Point course.

Several of my Air Force friends and I regularly took advantage of that opportunity, much to my wife's chagrin. She didn't mind the golf game, but wasn't enthused about our wanderings after the game. We would stop at bars on the way home for beers, and I would frequently call her from those bars to announce our progress on the way home. Clearly she would rather we came straight home from the course, but it was something we guys looked forward to most weekends. The designated driver always stayed sober, but the remaining three occasionally crossed the line.

Career military people always want to go where the action is and I was no different. During the summer of 1965 I went to a pay phone and called a contact at the Pentagon who handled Air Force public affairs assignments, and I volunteered to go to Vietnam. I used a pay phone because I didn't want anyone in my office to know that I was volunteering for my next assignment. But, as usual, the Air Force puts its needs ahead of individual wants and needs so I was transferred to the 13th Air Force on Clark Air Base in the Philippines.

13th Air Force, Clark Air Base, Republic of the Philippines

Toward the end of 1965, after nearly two years at Stewart AFB I was assigned to the 13th Air Force headquarters, in the Republic of the Philippines. As part of the 13th AF Public Affairs Office I ran a community relations program at bases in the Philippines, Thailand, and Taiwan, the 13th Air Force area of responsibility. I also scheduled performance tours of the 13th Air Force Band. My assignment was a 24-month accompanied tour of duty, but because of the scarcity of base housing, it would take nine months for the Air Force to allow Peggy to join me. Meanwhile I shared a house off base with several other Air Force officers.

I had transportation during that period because prior to moving its unit to Ben Hoa, Vietnam, the B-57 squadron was stationed at Clark Air Base in the Philippines. The unit would move to Ben Hoa for three or four months of temporary duty (TDY) and then rotate back to Clark Air Base. A B-57 pilot friend of mine loaned me his car to use at Clark whenever he went TDY to Vietnam. My own car would eventually be shipped to the Philippines, but I used my friend's car while he was flying in South Vietnam.

As part of my responsibilities I travelled a lot, visiting bases in all three areas of our command at least once each quarter so I could monitor how well our base community relations programs were functioning and to monitor public performances of the 13th Air Fore Band. This included coordinating all Air Force participation in an annual reenactment of the Leyte Landing in which General Douglas MacArthur returned to the Philippines during World War II. It required that I coordinate all Air Force participation, including aircraft flyovers, band participation, airlift for distinguished American military visitors, and coordination with the Philippine military and civilian officials. It took months to coordinate everything, but the reenactment was executed perfectly.

After a nine-month wait, my wife joined me at Clark Air Base and we set up residence in a nice rental house off base. Her arrival was amusing because it came in the midst of a torrential downpour so heavy that when she started to step off the aircraft, she couldn't see me standing at the foot of the ramp, so she turned to the Air Force steward and asked if someone could help her find her husband. It was an auspicious arrival. By then I was used to our monsoon season, but that kind of rain was a new experience for Peggy.

The first morning in our new house she was upset and cried because when she woke up and looked outside there were several water buffalo grazing in our yard. Someone had left open the gate to our property and a couple of water buffalo had wandered into our yard.

Peggy also found several large flying cockroaches in our house, which upset her even more. Of course cockroaches and other insects were not unusual in the Philippines. Over the next year there would be many other things that bothered her about living in the Philippines, not the least of which was the weather. It was very hot and humid and we did not have air conditioning, which meant we sometimes would lie almost naked on our terrazzo floors, which were the coolest places in the house.

The weather took some getting used to because we had never lived anywhere where there were only two seasons: wet and dry. Actually even the wet season was quite hot and humid. With the only options being sunshine or rain, we had to take some unusual steps to avoid mold in our shoes. We put lights along the base of the closet and left them on throughout the wet season so they would keep our shoes dry.

The wet season was unlike anything we had ever seen. It would sometimes rain for days. I remember one period in which we had a torrential downpour continuously for two weeks. During the rainy season we seemed to be wet constantly and driving wasn't easy. Sometimes the rain came down so hard the windshield wipers couldn't clear our windshield, and we would occasionally have to pull over to the side of the road and wait for the rain to lessen. Although Peggy loved her new friends, she was not a happy camper, but I loved my time in the Philippines. I loved the weather because hot and humid always appealed to me, I loved my assignment, including all the travel, and I loved meeting so many truly interesting people.

We had to get use to the different cultures. For instance in Thailand the head is the most sacred part of the body and the feet the least. It is an insult in Thailand to point your feet at another person, so I had to learn to keep my feet on the ground instead of crossing my legs like I might do at home. Also the King of Thailand is highly revered. Thailand is a constitutional monarchy, and the royal family is revered throughout the country. His image is everywhere, from posters plastered on the exterior of buildings to photos displayed on taxi dashboards. Everyone stands when the King's anthem is played before movies, concerts, and sporting events. Visitors to Thailand should never utter a disparaging remark about the royals. That is particularly important because strict laws apply, and offenses can be punishable by imprisonment.

There are important cultural differences in the Philippines too. Filipinos are very hospitable people. They always offer the best of whatever they have to their guests. If you happen to be in a Filipino house during dining hours, you will very likely be invited to the family meal. Regardless of what food they have or how much, regardless of who you are, they always invite their guest to eat and share whatever they have. Also, punctuality is nowhere nearly as important to them as it is to Americans. Filipino time is legend. Where we value punctuality they are notable for their tardiness.

Perhaps the most notable difference between the United States and Taiwan is that the Taiwanese are more group and family oriented, while Americans are more individual oriented. The Taiwanese are also more subtle and indirect in their communications. They prefer to drop hints and cues rather than being assertive and direct. They are also more reserved toward strangers and are less apt to smile or make eye contact until after they get to know you. They are taught to be modest, humble, and obedient rather than outspoken or assertive. In contrast, being quiet, submissive, and obedient is often seen as a weakness in the United States.

The good news about my Philippine assignment was that my secretary was the granddaughter of Emilio F. Aquinaldo, the president of the Philippines from 1899-1901, while the Philippines was still under Spanish rule, and she still had contacts at the highest level of the Philippine government. Ceffie was highly educated, with multiple master degrees, and knew all the politicians. She seemed like an ambassador for her country, in addition to being an excellent secretary. She was also a lovely woman, loved by everyone in our office.

I could never prove it, but I was certain she looked out for us the entire time we were in the Philippines. Most of the houses in our neighborhood were vandalized from time to time, but nobody ever bothered our house. While she would never admit it, I had no doubt that she somehow controlled the security around our house.

While assigned to 13th Air Force, I was promoted to captain and continued my public affairs duties. During my two years there I wrote most of the speeches given by both the 13th Air Force commander and vice commander, many of which were delivered with very positive results in front of international audiences. The 13th Air Force commander, Lt. Gen. Benjamin O. Davis, Jr., liked the speeches I wrote for him so much he insisted I write all of his speeches while he was there. So, in addition to my other duties I became the commander's speechwriter, a task I actually enjoyed. General Davis was an extraordinarily gifted speaker. He would reduce my speeches to 3" x 5" cards and hold them in the palm of his hand, all the while giving the illusion of the "first time," as though he was speaking extemporaneously. I've met very few senior executives who could do that convincingly.

I also monitored the staffing of 13th Air Force public affairs offices at two bases in the Philippines, six bases in Thailand, and two bases in Taiwan, all the while monitoring and supervising the base community relations programs at each of those bases. While some folks in our office complained about all the travel, I loved it. It was exciting to learn about the different cultures of each of the three regions that made up the 13th Air Force.

I also loved being assigned to Clark Air Base because it was absolutely beautiful. The base proper was set back five miles from the main gate and was literally covered with lush and beautiful vegetation. Most of the time I was there the base was abloom with magnificent flowers and extraordinary plants and gardens.

It was also a wonderful place to run and I began running seriously. While waiting for Peggy to join me in the Philippines, I started running about five miles per day and lost about 30 pounds. She thought it was probably from drinking and not eating well, but it was really from running. I fell in love with running and continued to run until I reached age 65. I was not competively fast, just persistent, and after a couple of years I was able to run eight miles every day. Sometimes people would ask me why I ran so much and my response was always: "Because I feel better on days that I run than I do on days I don't run."

I was smoking two packs of cigarettes per day while I was stationed in the Philippines and folks used to ask me how I could run as a smoker. My response was smoking didn't keep me from running; it just kept me from running fast. Later in life after I quit smoking, my running speed improved. While I was a smoker I ran 10 or 11-minute miles. After I quit smoking I ran 8-minute miles. My fasted running time was 6-minute miles. Running became a daily passion. I simply loved to run, but it was difficult to run every day while travelling.

Every time I went to Thailand I had a layover in Saigon to change airplanes, so I got a cursory look at Vietnam long before my future assignment there in 1974-1975. It was well known in the 1960s and 1970s that it was sometimes more dangerous in Saigon than at some of the bases around the country. That was not because we were under attack in the city, but because so many Americans let their guard down and felt safe when they left the really dangerous locations around the country. Some military members died their first day in country and some died their last day in country. Being in Saigon was a lot safer than being out in the field, but only if you were careful and didn't let your guard down.

I remember one time I was shaving in a hotel room when somebody outside fired an automatic weapon, and I could hear the shells hitting the building just outside an open window next to where I was shaving. I quickly picked up a towel, wiped off my face, turned to my roommate and said, " I don't think I'll shave just now."

At Clark we also had a wonderful Officer's Club, with cheap drinks, great bands, and impressive singers who could mimic international stars to the point you could close your eyes and not be able to tell the difference between the Filipino mimic and the real singer.

Mixed alcoholic drinks were embarrassingly cheap, as you might well expect them to be. You could buy a bottle of the best world-class bourbon or scotch for little more than two dollars. There was no federal tax on the alcohol. Of course we didn't overindulge. Not much. It's not a lie because my fingers are crossed.

My time with the 13th Air Force was fairly uneventful from a security standpoint. It was enjoyable, and I'll always remember how kind and considerate the local citizens were to Peggy and me. My two-year assignment to the 13th Air Force in the Philippines was a period in my life for which I will always have fond memories.

Boston University Graduate School

After two-years at 13th Air Force in the Philippines I was selected by the Air Force to attend a 12-month graduate program in public relations at Boston University (BU). It would lead to a Master of Science degree in Public Relations.

Keep in mind that I had earlier attended an Air Force short course in public relations at Boston University, that the Air Force subsequently moved to the University of Oklahoma after Boston University discontinued the short course to satisfy protesting students during uprisings in the early 1960s.

The assignment came as quite a surprise to me. I had expected to be assigned to another base somewhere in the United States, and I sure did not expect to be sent back to Boston University considering Air Force history with their short course. I didn't know it, but the Air Force had other plans for me.

Since I had already attended Boston University for the Air Force short course, I was familiar with the campus and the faculty, and felt comfortable navigating around the Boston area.

I also felt very privileged to be selected for this unique program. Each year the Air Force selected only four officers for its graduate program in public relations, which was great for our career field. The Air Force had and still has a stellar reputation for pubic affairs. While the other services have good programs too, their public affairs officers come from other career paths and move back and forth between career paths throughout their careers. In the Air Force a public affairs officer can spend his or her entire career in the public affairs career field, which is exactly what I did.

However, the atmosphere was a bit different when I returned home to the United States. Each generation of young people finds new ways to attract attention to their egocentric view of the world. I remember how surprised I was when I returned from the Philippines and Southeast Asia in 1968 to discover how dramatically the world had changed in my absence

After arriving back in the States, I was riding in a San Francisco bus when I saw a beautiful blonde in a car just ahead of us. Imagine my surprise when we pulled abreast of the car to find out the long, flowing, silky locks came with a mustache. It was my first experience with the androgynous look.

Later, in 1969, I was walking in Boston Commons when I came upon a young girl who stood out like a red rose in a bed of white carnations. She was dressed in combat boots, military fatigues, and a loose fitting sleeveless shirt, with green spiked hair and tattoos on both shoulders. She could have been a poster child for the "hippie" movement.

"What are you looking at," she snapped at me.

"I really didn't mean to stare," I said. "But, since you've worked so hard to call attention to yourself, it's not easy to believe your indignation is sincere." She flipped me the bird as she walked off.

Just as I was beginning to adapt to these unusual looks, along comes a new millennial custom: body piercing. It was one thing to see two or three holes in each ear for pierced earrings, but now it's not uncommon to see rings sticking through noses and cheeks, and even in eyebrows and tongues. I understand that today there are even piercings in more exotic parts of the body. There was a time you could only find that kind of self-mutilation in a National Geographic Magazine.

Sometimes the narcissistic craving for attention and/or the need to be part of a group drives young people to do things that defy the imagination. Nevertheless, I was glad to get home.

Peggy and I found a house to rent in Wellesley Hills, Massachusetts, with a trolley stop about two blocks from our house. Instead of driving to school, it was my plan to take the trolley to school every day. The trolley dropped me off two blocks from Boston University's College of Communication, which is where public relations is taught.

Here is what the university's web page says about its graduate course leading to a Master of Science in Public Relations program:

Welcome to the proud home of the world's first university degree in public relations. Other schools have followed suit, but we've never given up the lead. In our three-semester...program, you'll balance academics with practical application. You'll gain an overview of contemporary public relations, the nature of human communication, and the role of media before choosing an area of specialization. Hone your ability to write clearly and concisely in contemporary media formats, addressing different audiences. Develop professional management skills. And augment your studies with electives in nonprofit, corporate, or international pubic relations. When you're through, you'll be ready to assume a leadership role in public relations.

•　•　•

I can attest to the fact that our class sizes were small and much of the instruction was personal, including individual private time with professors who challenged us to think strategically as well as tactically. Since this was in fact my second time at Boston University, I didn't need a lot to time to scout around the campus or Boston, and I was already familiar with most of the graduate school professors.

It turned out I would study under a professor who became my all-time favorite teacher, including high school, undergraduate college, and graduate school. His name was Dr. Albert Sullivan. Today he would be called a progressive liberal professor who was the antithesis of what you might expect to find teaching Air Force officers. He tried to teach all of us to think "outside the box," to not be constrained by protocol or rules, which I found to be refreshing.

For instance, one of the courses he taught was writing, and he had the most unusual approach to punctuation I had ever seen—and I loved it. His writing philosophy was to throw out most, if not all, of the traditional writing rules taught in most high schools and colleges. His approach was basic and fundamental. Punctuation is not an inviolate set of rules to be slavishly followed. Punctuation is a form of traffic controls that tell the reader when to slow down, when to stop, when an associated explanation will be injected, when a series of related things will follow, and so forth. He had an explanation for everything from a comma, which tells the reader to slow down to a period, which tells the reader to come to a full stop, to a colon, which tells the reader that a series of related thoughts is coming, to a semi-colon, which tells the reader that an explanation or an example related to the basic sentence is coming. Every punctuation mark existed somewhere on a continuous spectrum to help the reader relate to whatever message the writer is trying to communicate.

Dr. Sullivan would say:

"Don't insert a comma just because some high school teacher told you a comma must be used at the beginning or end of a clause, or to connect two independent clauses, or to set off parenthetical elements. Throw out all the rules you were taught when you were young. Use punctuation to help the reader understand whatever it is you are trying to communicate. If you think the reader needs to stop to take a breath, put in a period. If the punctuation does for the reader whatever you intend for it to do, it is correct no matter what an English teacher says."

· · ·

I thoroughly enjoyed working with Dr. Sullivan, and he became my thesis advisor. One of the standard university requirements for a Master of Science degree was to write a thesis. I picked a topic early, based on my previous experience at the university. You will recall that Boston University threw the Air Force public affairs short course off campus during the mid-1960s because of all the student protests over the United States involvement in the Southeast Asian war. I chose as my thesis topic, "Campus Revolt: Violence vs. Non-violence. "

I did mostly periodical research during my first semester and wrote my thesis during the second semester. I competed my thesis project early and was ready for graduation. Many students never write their thesis; they delay doing it until it is too late to graduate. When asked about it, they'll say they will complete the research on their own time in between semesters and get back with the university when it's done. Regrettably, once the student leaves the campus, he or she generally gets caught up in the daily demands of whatever profession he or she practices to make a living and never finishes the thesis.

While social unrest was not a new phenomenon in the United States, student revolution on university campuses was new. During the 1960s student unwillingness to adapt to what they considered to be a "sick society not of their making" caused frustrations that were vented by attacking those systems on campus. They repeatedly rejected the values they didn't accept and that led to major student-administration confrontations throughout the county.

I examined four of those confrontations, two of which resulted in rioting and bloodshed. The University of California at Berkeley, Columbia University, Brandeis University, and Boston University each experienced a major crisis involving student take-over of one or more campus buildings, presentation of student demands, negotiation of the demands, and resolution of the crisis.

My thesis applied a well-known conceptual model based on universal preconditions to understand why riots occurred at two of the universities, while the other two resolved their crisis without violence. Both Brandies and Boston University featured administrators and students engaged in meaningful dialogue on campus without resorting to collective violence.

The key to successful negotiation whether between individuals, groups, or organizations is for both sides to be willing to really listen to each other. To truly listen, one must start with the basic assumption that one's opponent might just be right and the listener might just be wrong. That is a really tough proposition for most people. Far too often people don't really listen. When that happens there is every possibility that a shouting match will ensue, in which both sides are so engaged in "name-calling" that they don't even hear each other. Any side that starts with non-negotiable demands has already conceded defeat. Those demands preclude the possibility of conflict resolution through anything but complete acquiescence by one party or a contest of strength.

An explanation for the examples used in my thesis is far too long for this book. Indeed my thesis was 167 pages long. Suffice it to say my thesis was well received by Boston University's Communications Department.

I finished my graduate courses almost as a straight "A" student, but I made a serious mistake. I had miscalculated and finished all of my course requirements for graduation one semester early. That meant I had to select another course to occupy me during that last semester. It occurred to me that I might benefit by taking an international course because I had no idea where my next assignment might be. So I mistakenly took an intelligence course on the Soviet Union instead of another course on public relations. Big mistake! Almost all of the other students had majored in Russian, Russian history, or both. I had no foundation in anything even associated with the Soviet Union. The consequence was that I struggled mightily, and the professor graciously gave me a "B" for the course. I was lost most of the time that other students felt right at home.

When my time at Boston University was concluded, in addition to my Master of Science degree in public relations, I also had accumulated 10 hours towards a doctorate. I chose to not invest any more effort towards a doctorate when I discovered that in the corporate world the master's degree is the terminal degree. I would learn that the doctorate is generally only of significant value to teachers and scientists.

Peggy and I had an enjoyable time living in Wellesley Hills. However, I was surprised to learn that being accepted by Bostonians when one comes from out of state is not easy. Our neighbors mostly ignored us until winter came, with its huge snowstorms and nearly impassable streets. Two of our neighbors were elderly and somewhat infirmed, so after the first snowfall, I voluntarily shoveled their sidewalks and driveways. After that I could do no wrong. The rest of our time in Wellesley Hills was delightful.

Incidentally, it was while I was attending Boston University that Neil Armstrong and Buzz Aldrin first walked on the moon. I mistakenly thought I could capture a photo of their landing by photographing it from the television. Of course the flash from my camera completely washed out the picture. I felt incredibly foolish for not remembering that would happen. Even so, it was one day in the life of my time in the Boston area I will never forget.

Back to the Pentagon

I was astonished to get my next assignment. It was a return to the Pentagon where I was assigned as an action officer to the Secretary of the Air Force Office of Public Affairs, News Media Relations Division, Magazines and Books Branch. My principal job was to serve as a credible point of contact for Air Force authors and the national news media, particularly the national magazine field and national book publishers.

When I returned to the Pentagon I was surprised to learn that the building was no longer open to the general public. When I had previously served in naval intelligence during the 1950s, anybody in the entire world could just walk into the Pentagon and browse around the corridors.

That had changed because during the early 1960s Vietnam War protestors had gained access to the Pentagon and planted explosives, blowing up several restrooms. In 1967 more than 50,000 protestors marched against the Pentagon, and even after I returned there in 1969, protestors surrounded the Pentagon and locked their arms in an effort to keep civilian and military personnel who worked there from entering the building.

I remember one time when I had to literally break through locked arms to get into the Pentagon after being called bizarre names for serving in the military, many of which were so profane I dare not repeat them here. I remember telling a group of protestors, mostly young demonstrators, that they were in the wrong place.

I explained that people who work in the Pentagon are patriotic public servants, who are defending the demonstrator's right to "free speech." Pentagon employees and the military do not decide which wars we fight, I explained. People working in the Pentagon do not make those decisions. Those decisions were made by civilian authorities who reside at 1600 Pennsylvania Avenue (the White House) or work on Capital Hill (the Congress). I explained that the protestors achieved nothing by blocking entrances to the Pentagon.

They were not impressed by my explanations; they were having too much fun exercising their free speech rights, even though blocking entrance to the Pentagon was a crime, not an expression of free speech.

By the 1970s only people with a government identification card could freely enter the Pentagon. Anyone else who wanted to enter would have to arrange for someone who worked there to vouch for him or her by meeting the visitor at the entrance and escorting the visitor to the appropriate destination for his or her meeting.

As an aside, today the Pentagon's visitor policy is even more strict. Even visitors who have a military identification card cannot just walk into the Pentagon. They must be met by someone who has legitimate access and be escorted to whatever office they intend to visit. The last time I visited the Pentagon in the 1990s to legitimately talk to someone I had business with, I had to get my contact to come to the River Entrance and escort me to his office, even though I am a retired Air Force lieutenant colonel who at one time had a Top Secret clearance, and had previously served for seven years in the Pentagon. They simply have much tighter visitor controls today than they had in the past.

As part of my job I would contact public affairs representatives at our major air commands, such as Tactical Air Command or Strategic Air Command, or Military Airlift Command or Pacific Air Command to see if they had any story ideas that might make for an interesting article from a civilian perspective. Each command had many of divisions, groups, or squadrons that were unique to our Air Force mission and might serve as the basis for stories to tell that would be of interest to the general public. I was in touch with a variety of nationally or regionally circulated magazines that had varied editorial needs to fill every month or quarter. It was my job to serve as a bridge between our commands and the magazines.

I would ask my contacts to submit their ideas for articles of various lengths, such as 2,000-5,000-word articles. I would take their ideas and build a two or three sentence story idea that I thought might interest a general audience and submit it to a magazine editor offering exclusivity. We never floated story ideas to multiple editors at the same time because of potential conflicts if more than one wanted the story. Besides, offering exclusivity was an added incentive to appeal to an editor.

Once an editor indicated some positive interest, even if it was a guarantee to seriously consider the article, rather than a publication commitment, I would ask the major command public affairs officer to ask their author or authors to prepare the article and submit it directly to me. Usually the articles were about some facet of our Air Force mission, usually something that involved daily participation of our personnel.

It was always helpful to select authors who were talented at crafting stories about their work environment in terms to which civilian audiences could relate. I would then review the article for suitability, and if suitable, I would submit it to the OASD/PA security review office for classification clearance. We couldn't risk the possibility of offering an article for publication that might include classified data.

Once cleared, I would submit the article to the magazine editor. Most of the time if an article made it through our process and the editor had already indicated an interest in the story idea, publication was almost certain. It was just another way to show the civilian population how they benefited from our Air Force programs.

I remember one six-month period during 1970 in which we increased our story idea submissions by 31 percent, which generated 67 articles in magazines having a combined circulation of 57 million readers. At the same time I was helping my contacts generate story ideas that might also appeal to book publishers. Sometimes that required a concentrated and dedicated focus on research of documents to identify releasable information of interest to a specific book author.

During 1971, for a period of one year we generated 161 feature articles that were published in nationally circulated magazines. During that year I had a 50 percent acceptance rate, which increased our visibility among the reading public. I consistently placed 10 or more articles every month in magazines such as *Popular Mechanics, V.F.W., True, Business Week, Fortune, Reader's Digest, U.S. News and World Report,* and an assortment of others too numerous to mention in their entirety.

During 1973 I was responsible for placing 258 Air Force articles in nationally circulated magazines, which was more than those published in 1970 and 1971 combined, and we responded to more than 300 inquiries from magazine and book editors about Air Force topics, some of which were related to sensitive information that could not be released. The important but sometimes difficult task was to be able to explain to editors how much their inquiries were appreciated, even when we were not able to release the information they wanted.

In addition to our focus on magazine articles, I assisted the authors of books such as the biographies of "Hap" Arnold and Jimmy Doolittle, and a book titled *The Story of the B-29.* I also had my personal by-lined articles about the Air Force included in *Air Line Pilot* magazine and the *World Book Encyclopedia.*

I spent a considerable amount of time helping David Westheimer, the noted author of the immensely successful novel *Von Ryan's Express*, which was later made into a popular movie starring Frank Sinatra. I helped Westheimer research World War II records to find data that would support his major book project *Lighter Than a Feather.* While that book was a work of fiction, it included a 36-page epilogue, which in the second printing became a 36-page prologue that set the fact-based stage for the work of fiction. Which is to say it meticulously set the stage as it actually existed just prior to our dropping the atom bomb on Hiroshima, Japan. It presupposed that the Allies would launch an invasion of the Japanese homeland.

The novel was written from the perspective of what would have been required had the United States not dropped the atomic bombs on Hiroshima and Nagasaki, causing Japan to agree to an unconditional surrender. The novel was based on the real world military plans, Operation Olympic (the planned invasion of Japan by the Allies) and Operation Ketsu-Go (the Japanese plan to defend their homeland).

Westheimer structured the book so alternate chapters informed the reader from the perspective of the Allied and Japanese participants throughout the conclusion of the fictional conflict.

My role was to help David Westheimer, who much later became a very close friend of mine, research military records so he could accurately depict the setting that existed just before the atomic bombs were dropped, when Allied forces were about to invade Japan.

This provocative piece of speculative fiction was based on meticulous research and subsequent downgrading of classified records so Westheimer could use the materials in his book. The research and security review took several months, and *Lighter Than a Feather* became a very successful novel.

While serving in this position I was promoted to major and offered a regular Air Force commission, an enviable recognition of my contribution to the Air Force, which my former supervisor at Retail Credit Company had predicted would never happen. Of course I accepted the regular commission while I continued with my Magazine and Book Branch duties.

During my time in the Magazine and Book Branch I continued to write articles of my own that were published in major magazines, even as I continued helping magazine and book authors throughout the Air Force. Late in 1974 my supervisor estimated that coverage the Air Force received from my efforts over the five years I had spent in this branch writing and helping other authors to get published accounted for more than $40 million of advertising exposure for the Air Force, which resulted in the award of an Air Force Commendation Medal to me as my tenure in the Pentagon came to a close.

My next assignment to the Joint Casualty Resolution Center (JCRC) with headquarters at the Nakhon Phanom Royal Thai Air Force Base, Thailand, was equally surprising.

Joint Casualty Resolution Center (JCRC)

For those readers who may not be familiar with JCRC, it was the Department of Defense joint organization tasked with the responsibility for locating those Americans who had been declared Missing In Action (MIA) during their involvement in the war in South Vietnam. Little was known about where they were or if they had died in combat, and if so, what the disposition was of their remains. In essence, the MIAs were men who had died in combat, but whose bodies had never been recovered.

JCRC consisted of about 80 percent Army Special Forces (Green Berets), 15 percent Army Mortuary Affairs specialists, and five percent people like me from the other services. An Army brigadier general commanded JCRC and an Air Force colonel was the deputy. It was the task of the Special Forces to protect us, while the Mortuary Affairs specialists exhumed the remains of the MIAs once we found them.

My job as the JCRC public affairs officer was to be the single point of contact with the international news media to answer their inquiries and to explain to the American public what our mission was and how successful we were in recovering the remains of those Americans who had died in combat but who had never been recovered. Part of my job included accompanying search and recovery teams throughout South Vietnam to serve as the unit focus for news media who might show up at the recovery sites.

At the time of my assignment there were still 2,400 American military members who had been killed in action in South Vietnam, Cambodia, and Laos but whose bodies had never been recovered. The current military claim that we never leave anyone behind must be clarified. We never knowingly or intentionally leave anyone behind; however, the sad truth is that during intensive conflicts in which everyone in a military unit may be killed, there may be no immediate accounting for those bodies.

For instance, after a firefight in a contested area, which may well have been the backyard of a local citizen, the remains of deceased combatants could become a health hazard in just a few days. So, sometimes the local residents would dig a large hole and place all the comingled bodies in a mass grave and cover them with soil. I'll explain more about that later.

What many people don't know is that counting World War II, the Korean War, and the Vietnam War, there were more than 80,000 men and women who were listed as MIAs for many years. However, we never stopped looking for them; so, according to the POW-MIA web page, that number has since been reduced to 40,401 missing from World War II, Korea, and Vietnam combined.

Since I served in JCRC from July 1974 – July 1975, the 2,400 figure for Vietnam has been reduced to 1,719 because of the efforts of JCRC and its successor organization, the Joint Task Force-Full Accounting Office (JTF-FA) which is located in Camp H.M. Smith, Hawaii, with detachments in Thailand,

Vietnam, and Laos.

The truth is that these figures will never be reduced to zero because some pilots, particularly Navy pilots, were shot down and crashed into the ocean. Some pilots, mostly Air Force and Army pilots, were shot down and crashed into double and triple canopied jungles in Vietnam, Laos, and Cambodia. It is unlikely these Americans, mostly aircrews, will ever be recovered. But, as I noted earlier, we will never stop looking for them. On the other hand some men and women will never be recovered because they were incinerated in massive explosions. I remember one case where a young Marine was sitting next to an ammunition dump when an enemy round hit the dump. The Marine's body was vaporized from the explosion, and there will never be anything left of him to recover.

Forty-one years after the Vietnam War, we are still trying to find more than 1,700 Americans who didn't come home. I have a special appreciation for Department of Defense personnel who are searching for them. I know that JCRC had an information program in which its members reached out to individual villages with flyers and other communication tools, including coordination with the local State Department's Consulate Generals Office, to gather casualty resolution data and to let the villagers know that we are interested in any information they may have about where Americans might be buried. A lot of the information JCRC tracked and followed up on came from villagers.

Of the 30 years I served in the United States military, the assignment I treasured the most was the year I spent with the JCRC.

For more than a year I accompanied search and recovery teams in much of South Vietnam where we looked for, located, and exhumed American remains, which we took to our Central Identification Laboratory where they could be identified. Sometimes recovering those remains involved unique hazards, and whenever I was in either Saigon or Bangkok, the American embassy information people were glad I was in town.

For as long as I was in either city the embassies had all casualty resolution questions channeled to me so they wouldn't have to deal with them. Whenever I was out in the field in South Vietnam I wasn't available to the embassies, because I was always handling inquiries from the international news media who invariably came to the excavation site where we were working.

For the first year of its operation JCRC notified members of the Four Party Joint Military Team (FPJTM) to let them know where we would be located in

South Vietnam looking for our MIAs. The FPJMT consisted of representatives from the United States, South Vietnam, the Viet Cong, and North Vietnam.

Since JCRC was a humanitarian organization, its members were not allowed to carry weapons. The closest thing to a weapon each of us carried was a survival knife with a six-inch blade. If we needed to clear a landing zone for a helicopter, we could not use explosives to clear the ground. We had to use chain saws to cut down the trees. The international orange patches we wore on our shoulders and chests substantiated the fact that our teams were unarmed humanitarian military members.

In December 1973, about six months before I arrived, the Viet Cong ambushed one of the JCRC field teams led by Captain Richard Rees. As usual, JCRC had notified all four FPJMT member nations of where we would be conducting our search. It was standard conduct for us to let them know where we would be.

Captain Rees and his unarmed team were at the mercy of the automatic weapons fire that the Viet Cong ambushers raked across the paddy field. Rees and his men threw themselves down into the knee-deep water, hoping that the weeds and old paddy dikes would provide some degree of cover from the ambushers' fire. Captain Rees quickly realized that they were totally at the mercy of their attackers. In a final courageous gamble to save his team, Rees stood up with his hands raised, and shouted in Vietnamese to the attackers to stop their firing because his men were unarmed. A volley of fire immediately answered his shout from the brush at the edge of the paddy, and Captain Rees fell dead in the water.

The Viet Cong quickly withdrew from the scene leaving behind one American killed and four team members wounded, one Vietnamese killed and three wounded, and one helicopter destroyed. From that day forward we no longer notified the Viet Cong or the North Vietnamese whenever our teams were on a casualty resolution mission in the field.

Nevertheless, we continued to notify our South Vietnamese partners whenever we had a field mission. Unfortunately, wanting to impress the United States with how much they cooperated with JCRC in the recovery of our MIAs, the South Vietnamese would let the local and international news media know the location of our field trips. The consequence was that international reporters always met us at the site of our exhumations.

It was my job to handle the reporters and photographers. I would first let them know that they could take pictures until we unearthed the remains of our dead MIAs, at which time they would have to stop taking pictures. We did not want photographs of dead bodies and/or badly decomposed bodies to appear in newspapers around the world. We were very concerned about the sensitivities of the next-of-kin.

In the United States, Air Force public affairs officers have very limited control over what reporters can do at crash sites. In South Vietnam I took extraordinary measures to control the photographers, even standing in front of their cameras when necessary to keep them from taking pictures. We simply insisted they not photograph exhumed remains.

Some sites had unique hazards. One day, after opening a mass gravesite in Hue, where Vietnamese and American casualties had been buried together after a firefight, our mortuary affairs specialists discovered that ammunition and grenades were still attached to the bodies.

A fierce battle had been fought in and around Hue during the 1968 Tet offensive, and to avoid health hazards, local citizens quickly buried many casualties from both sides of the conflict in mass graves.

Because the commingled bodies had been buried for about six years, the grenades and ammunition could have been highly volatile. Having remained so long in one place, the chemicals in the grenades could have pooled and become sensitive to movement, so I ordered our men to get out of the gravesite until a Vietnamese explosive ordnance disposal (EOD) team could arrive to clear the site of all munitions. I was the senior officer present for that exhumation, as was often the case.

It was a really tough situation for my Vietnamese counterpart because the closest Vietnam EOD team was many miles from our site, and it could not reach us until sometime the next day. After about 15 minutes, my Vietnamese counterpart turned to one of his enlisted men and said something I couldn't hear.

The Vietnamese soldier then jumped into the gravesite, took off the hand grenades, and threw them a considerable distance, at which point they each exploded. Because of their volatility the munitions could have exploded the moment he touched them.

I learned a valuable lesson that day about cultural differences in how we value and respect life. I would never have put any soldier at risk to avoid an inconvenient delay. My choice would have been to keep our mortuary affairs specialists out of the gravesite until the EOD team cleared the site.

Throughout the years I have been asked many times if serving with JCRC was depressing work because of constant proximity to our military men who had died in combat. It was not! It was one of the most important and most satisfying jobs I ever had in the military, because each time we identified a serviceman whose remains we had recovered, one more family could stop wondering if he was alive or dead. That was terribly important because it is unbearable for a family to not know what happened to its loved one. We helped bring closure to grieving families, and nothing else I ever did in the military could compare with that.

In addition to bringing closure to the families of remains we recovered and identified, we did everything we could to help family members of those MIAs we had not yet found. A few of the next-of-kin came to South Vietnam at their own expense just to walk where their loved one had last been seen. Sometimes it was particularly poignant because the grieving spouse would throw her arms around a JCRC member and plead with him for any information we might be able to provide about efforts to locate her husband or son. We did everything we could to comfort the grieving family member. We provided everything we could, short of divulging classified information, but it was not the same as locating a set of remains.

Military families who still have relatives who were declared missing in action during the Vietnam conflict, as well as previous and subsequent wars, need to know that the Department of Defense POW/Missing Personnel Office will never quit looking for them. The extreme passage of time reduces the probability of finding them, but we never give up hope that one day we may recover and identify them, or at the very least gather concrete evidence of what happened to them. Even many years after World War II, a Japanese soldier occasionally came walking out of the jungle somewhere in the Philippines. Massive news media coverage of such an event gives hope to surviving American families that some day their loved one may also come walking out of a jungle in Southeast Asia. Sometimes families hold on to that hope until we are able to recover the remains of their missing spouse or child.

During every war, some of our military members just disappear until we can gather evidence that pinpoints their last location. At the risk of being redundant, I repeat that finding our men and women who are still missing is one of our nation's highest priorities. It is an eternal search that will never stop as long as even one

American is unaccounted for.

You might ask, how do we find them? How do you find and identify bodies, especially those who have been deceased and missing for a very long time, or were buried in an unidentified field or both?

The process is more detailed, complex, and interesting than anything we see today in television programs like '"CSI" or "NCIS." When JCRC members learned of a potential crash or burial site, often from local Vietnamese residents who helped bury them or knew someone who had participated in the burial, a JCRC team began culling through military command records.

The military maintains detailed records of its subordinate units and the men and women who served in those units. Before an individual can be specifically identified, he or she must be placed into an identifiable group to begin winnowing down the possibilities.

A forensic pathologist who specializes in identifying human remains can fairly quickly determine if the skeletal remains are Southeast Asian Mongloid or more likely North American Caucasoid or Negroid.

In a humid climate such as Vietnam, most remains quickly become skeletal, and a forensic pathologist can often determine the general area of the world from which the remains came.

For instance, Vietnamese skeletal remains are generally much smaller than American remains, and Vietnamese leg bones are dramatically different than American leg bones because the Vietnamese spend so much of their life squatting.

Once the remains are determined to likely be American, the JCRC team correlates information gleaned from major command records to determine if there was ever a service member declared MIA in the general area of the site in which the remains were found.

Thereafter the physical characteristics of those missing are compared to the characteristics of the skeletal remains that helps determine the general age, height, weight, sex, and nationality of individuals from which a match may be made. Specific characteristics from medical and dental records are then compared to those from the skeleton.

DNA evidence is best; however, when that is not available, dental records are often quite helpful if a portion of the jaw is recovered. But equally valuable is the recovery of a skull. A procedure known as Craniofacial Superimposition Technique (CFS) is considered to be nearly as reliable as fingerprints.

Bio Portfolio reports that CFS is an important way of identifying individuals when there is no DNA or reliable dental records available. The technique involves comparing the skull with a portrait photograph of an individual.

A photograph is taken of the skull, which produces a negative. That negative is then superimposed over a negative of the portrait photograph. If the facial characteristics match, identification is almost certain. The specific location of the eyes, nose, and mouth of one person is almost as unique as fingerprints.

If DNA, dental records, or a skull are not available, a more detailed forensic pathological analysis of remains must be used. It can take weeks, sometimes even months or years to positively identify a specific individual. Certainly it would be extremely rare for someone to be identified in days or a week as it happens on "CSI" or "NCIS." Television and movie producers take great liberty with facts to create drama and to resolve cases within a specified time constraint.

Today the search for and identification of our MIAs continues by a successor organization to JCRC and the DOD Central Identification Laboratory, both of which are located in Hawaii.

According to www.MIAFacts.org there are still over 1,606 MIAs from the Vietnam War. The JTF-FA staff in Hawaii and their branch offices are still gathering data from Vietnam as they continue their searches.

JCRC only existed for three years, 1973-1976, but the data they gathered and their work continues today with their successor the JTF-FA, which continues to conduct field operations in specific areas in which we believe there is a possibility of finding the remains of Americans.

During the course of my year assigned to JCRC, the United States Embassy in Saigon specifically requested that I be assigned to handle all matters, particularly news media and pubic inquiries, related to casualty resolution. During that period I personally participated in formal ceremonies when our government took possession of remains turned over by the South Vietnamese government.

Throughout my tenure at JCRC, I also coordinated requests for the JCRC commander to speak in front of visiting groups of distinguished Congressional representatives, and prepared the commander's remarks and speeches. This was particularly important when distinguished guests visited our embassies in Saigon and Bangkok.

One consequence of my time in South Vietnam wasn't expected. While most

Americans assigned to bases in Vietnam spent their entire year of duty at one base or in one location, I accompanied search and recovery teams all over the country. In the course of my travels I passed through a lot of areas that had been sprayed with Agent Orange. At the time I didn't think anything about it. Agent Orange was an excellent defoliant that cleared combat areas. Unfortunately we didn't know at that time what insidious health hazards emanated from that particular chemical.

In 1989 I had a massive heart attack that nearly killed me. I almost died three times. But, while I survived, it destroyed the bottom half of my heart, so I live with only half a heart, which means my heart cannot provide enough oxygenated blood and I tire very quickly with minimal exertion. I'm a perfect example of how you can survive a major heart attack with good doctors, the latest technology, and great medicines. Nevertheless, I have to be careful how much physical exertion I use.

In addition to that I am an insulin-dependent diabetic and the effect of that is that I have neuropathy in both feet, which causes discomfort when I walk. I survive with both of these conditions, but I have to be more careful than I might otherwise have had to be.

According to the Veteran's Administration all of these conditions were caused by my exposure to Agent Orange. Nevertheless, if I had it to do it again I would still serve with JCRC because of the good we did for grieving families. It was, without any doubt, the highlight of my military career.

My tour with JCRC came to a close in 1975 as the United States was withdrawing from South Vietnam. I still look back on that year with much fondness. I developed a great respect for the Army Green Berets and the Mortuary Affairs specialists. They are some of the finest men serving in our armed forces. That assignment also gave me a new appreciation for how well men and women from different services can work together in a common goal. It is amazing how quickly the color of a uniform is ignored when soldiers, sailors, and airmen all work together to achieve the same outcome.

Much to my surprise for my next assignment I was sent to the National War College (NWC) at Fort McNair, in Washington, D.C. However, I wasn't assigned there as a student, but as its public affairs officer, which meant I would continue to work in a joint service environment.

National Defense University

Two armed forces war colleges sit across the street from each other on Fort Lesley J. McNair: the National War College and the Industrial College of the Armed Forces. When I arrived they were each separate and distinct, with their own support operations, including departments in a variety of disciplines such as administration, academic, personnel, photographic, public affairs, and transportation.

Fort McNair is a U.S. Army post located on the tip of Greenleaf Point, the peninsula that lies at the confluence of the Potomac and the Anacostia Rivers in Washington, D.C. The fort has been an Army post for more than 200 years, third in length of service after the United States Military Academy at West Point and Carlisle Barracks in Pennsylvania, which is home to the U.S. Army War College. Fort McNair is historic and beautiful.

I was assigned to be the National War College public affairs officer working for and reporting directly to the college commandant, Vice Admiral (three-stars) Marmaduke G. Bayne, USN, who I came to respect as much as any military officer for whom I had ever worked. It was not just that he was a great officer, role model and genuinely good man; he was simply one of the most impressive men I had ever met.

Admiral Bayne served as the National War College commandant from 1972-1976, at which time he became the first President of the newly created National Defense University (NDU), which consisted of the National War College and the Industrial College of the Armed Forces.

My staff consisted of just a secretary. The first thing I did after familiarizing myself with the college, its curriculum, and students was to contact *The Washington Post* about running a feature article on the National War College, which it did in a Sunday issue. It was a major piece that covered the National War College as a huge national asset. It caught the faculty and students by surprise.

Nothing like that had been done for many years, and Admiral Bayne was very pleased with the exposure it generated in the greater Washington, DC area, which included the Pentagon, the Office of the Secretary of Defense, the Joint Chiefs of Staff, the Service Secretaries, the State Department, and a plethora of other military and government bureaus and departments, many of whose representatives had attended the National War College or the Industrial College of the Armed

Forces as students. Admiral Bayne called me into his office and let me know he had been trying to get such an article in the *Washington Post* ever since he had been appointed as the commandant

I also introduced our staff and students to what was the Air Force Hometown News Program. It is a program in which I sent a news release to the Hometown News Center about student attendance at, graduation from, or both, from the National War College. The Hometown News Center in turn sent news releases to newspapers in the student's hometown area announcing his or her attendance and graduation from one of our nation's premier war colleges. The program excited the students because they were all, as far as I could tell, proud to have been selected to attend and graduate from the National War College. It would be recognized as a great asset to them in their career development.

While I didn't know it at the time, the Department of Defense and the Joint Chiefs of Staff had decided to merge the National War College and the Industrial College of the Armed Forces into a university concept in which all the support functions for the two colleges, which had previously been independent, would come together to bridge the two colleges as one organization to be known as the National Defense University (NDU).

Combining all the support functions made it possible to consolidate the tasks and eliminate the redundancies by structuring one administrative overlay that supported both colleges. It also saved a lot of money for the Joint Chiefs of Staff that could be devoted to other responsibilities.

The National War College commandant had been selected to become the first president of the National Defense University and he had identified four other people he wanted to be part of his five-man planning staff to create the new university.

Admiral Bayne put together a planning staff that included a State Department ambassador as his vice president, an Army colonel as his operations officer, a retired Navy captain as his administrator and me as his public affairs officer. I was quite pleased to be part of this select group of people to create a new Department of Defense joint educational operation to be known as the National Defense University.

According to The National War College web page, it was and still is a senior-level course of instruction in national security strategy. Its mission is to prepare future leaders of the Armed Forces, State Department, and other civilian agencies for high-level policy, command, and staff responsibilities by conducting a senior-level course of study in national security strategy and national security policy.

In furtherance of this mission, the college curriculum focuses on grand strategy – the integration of all elements of national power – as well as the theory and practice of war, fundamentals of strategic thinking for national security matters, the global security arena, the inter-agency decision-making process, contemporary military strategy, and joint and combined warfare.

A fundamental strength of the college is its joint environment and approach. Students and faculty are drawn from all of the armed services and from civilian departments and agencies concerned with national security policies. The college program stresses thinking less parochially and more jointly in military planning and operations and the interrelationship of domestic, foreign, and defense policy.

The Industrial College of the Armed Forces, located across the street from the National War College, prepares selected military officers and civilians for leadership roles by conducting executive-level instruction` with associate studies in national power, materiel acquisition and joint logistics, and their integration into national security strategy for war and peace. ICAF grants to its graduates a Master of Science degree in National Resource Strategy.

ICAF was established in 1924 and focused on wartime procurement and mobilization procedures. In 1946 it was named the Industrial College of the Armed Forces and was reconstituted as a joint educational institution under the direction of the Joint Chiefs of Staff, effectively making it a multi-service military institution.

The two colleges were incorporated into the National Defense University in 1976 when the latter was created as the country's pre-eminent joint professional military education center.

Unfortunately shortly after the university was created Admiral Bayne developed bladder cancer and had to retire. Lieutenant General (three stars) Robert (Bobby) G. Gard, USA, became the next university president, and I worked for him during the next five years.

I tell you so much about the two colleges to help you understand the environment I initially faced in my new assignment. From a public affairs perspective one of the first issues I had to deal with was the first graduation of students from the university. It was a public relations problem because my major job was to promote the establishment of the university, and while many students were proud of their attendance at one of the colleges, they weren't interested in being associated with the new university.

For instance, at graduation time a student would say to me "I don't want any mention of the university in news releases about my graduation. I am going to be a graduate of the National War College and I want that to be the focus, not this new gimmick called the National Defense University. Nobody even knows what the hell that is!"

I had the same problem with ICAF students. While the number of students who had a negative attitude about the university was small, it was nevertheless a thorn in my side to deal with, and I included information about the new university in each hometown news release anyway. It was simply a reality the students had to deal with. As time passed and new classes were assigned to the two colleges, newer students became accustomed to the concept of attending and graduating from the NDU as well as their individual college, and the problem simply diminished over time.

Another university assignment I cherished was unexpected. The university president selected me to represent him by attending a variety of lectures, seminars, panels, and case studies at both colleges to observe and report back to him my judgments of the value of those academic programs to the students.

Incidentally, all lectures at the two colleges are conducted under a strict "no quotation nor attribution" policy that has facilitated discussion on some of the most difficult issues of the day. A violation of the non-attribution policy is considered to be a serious breach of protocol that could have serious repercussions for a student.

In addition to my function as the university spokesman, responsible for contact with the local, regional, and national news media and the general public, I was selected to assist a faculty member in teaching a course titled "The Commander and the Media." The course drew on my experiences as a public affairs officer while handling major Air Force aircraft accidents in the public domain. I responded with real world answers to student questions about how a commander should relate to public inquiries if an aircraft in his command crashes into an off-base public domain.

The course included a considerable amount of role-playing in which the students assumed the role of a base commander who had to deal with reporters following an aircraft accident in the vicinity of his base, but still in the public arena. In the role-playing exercises I pretended to be a reporter asking them serious questions they could be expected to get in a real world situation. It was an eye opener for the students who were used to being able to control their environment but had very little control in this scenario. Some of them did well and some not so well, but it was a great learning experience for all of them.

To give you some appreciation for the level and quality of NDU students, alumni include graduates who became distinguished leaders, such as: General Colin Powell, Senator John McCain, former NATO Supreme Allied Commander- Europe Wesley Clark, former U.S. Army Chief of Staff Peter Pace, former U.S. Chief of Naval Operations Elmo Zumwalt, and former Commandant of the Marine Corps Robert H. Barrow. I could fill this page with the names of illustrious military and civilian leaders who have attended one of the two colleges at NDU, but I'm sure you get the picture.

My initial assignment to the National War College was for a four-year period, and it carried over to my assignment at the National Defense University. However, General Gard was very pleased with my performance, and fought with the Air Force to get my assignments extended, and I eventually served at the college and university for six years. During that time I got a good senior service college education myself. Also, while at the university I was promoted to lieutenant colonel.

Another wonderful benefit of my assignment at NDU was the fact that both colleges had racquetball courts, and I was able to hone my racquetball skills over a long period. As immodest as it sounds, while I played against students, faculty, and staff, I never lost a game in the six years I was there. Keep in mind that a match is the best two out of three games, and I never lost a single game, which means I never lost a single match in six years. My boss was shocked that he could not beat me. While I had no way to know for sure, I always suspected that some other competitors who were junior in rank occasionally let him win, or to be charitable backed off their game. I took pride in my racquetball skills, and I never ever let anyone beat me. If a competitor won it was because he played better than me, not because I slacked off and let him win.

So you don't think otherwise, I did not have a "big head" over racquetball. I never gloated and always praised my opponent's efforts. Each match was a new challenge for me, and I never ever took my games for granted. I was constantly surprised at my evolving skill level on the courts, even though there was no end to the number of students challenging me to a match. Once word got out that I was difficult to beat, lots of men wanted to try.

With back-to-back joint assignments I was reminded once again how well the separate and different services can work together on a common goal. My time at the university was a wonderful experience that still gives me pleasure when I think about it. My next assignment would be dramatically different.

Air Force Public Affairs—Western Region

After serving six years at the NDU I was selected to replace the Air Force colonel who had been in charge of the Secretary of the Air Force public affairs office for the western United States. My office was located on the 10th floor of the Federal Building in Westwood, which is a commercial and residential neighborhood in the north central portion of the western region of Los Angeles, California. It is also where the Westwood Village Memorial Park Cemetery and the University of California at Los Angeles are located.

Our office complex occupied a suite of rooms to accommodate a staff of six professionals who represented the Air Force in public affairs, as well as internal and community relations' activities throughout the western United States.

During the three years I served in this Los Angeles office, while I supervised our responsibilities as they related to support of Air Force base public affairs offices throughout the 11 west coast states, we mostly served as the primary Los Angeles public affairs support to the Secretary of the Air Force and other senior Department of Defense and Air Force military and civilian leaders.

During this time I coordinated support for Secretary of Defense and Secretary of the Air Force speaking engagements at major events in key California cities such as San Diego, San Francisco, and Los Angeles and responded to news media inquiries that involved those high-level dignitaries. I was also the Air Force's focal point for handling sensitive public and news media inquiries and for writing articles about the nuclear freeze issues. Nuclear freeze was a really hot issue between 1982 and1984.

Nuclear Freeze Issue

During October 1982 I supported Charlton Heston when he engaged in face-to-face debates with Paul Newman on national television over the nuclear freeze issue. I supported Heston by delivering factual data for him to use in his opposition to the proposed nuclear freeze. His position was that a nuclear freeze would preserve in place the nuclear superiority enjoyed by the Soviet Union. Newman's stated position in favor of a nuclear freeze was that before an arms race could be stopped, it first had to be frozen in place. The two of them publicly debated the issue over a period of months.

During this period I got to see a side of Charlton Heston most Americans rarely have a chance to see. He had a wonderful sense of humor and was gracious to everyone. He seemed to really appreciate everything I did to help him prepare for his debates with Paul Newman. I will forever remember my first visit to Heston's home, which was sometimes described as "the house that Ben Hur built." He lived in a beautiful hilltop estate on Coldwater Canyon, in Beverly Hills. His home included stunning mountain views from most of its rooms and a spectacular two-story library located off the master suite.

The first time I drove up to his three-acre property, which included a huge driveway, a massive brute of a dog approached my car and met me with a menacing growl. I was hesitant to get out of the car because I feared he might attack me, so I sat there for a few minutes and just blew my horn.

Pretty soon Heston came out of his house, walked up to my car laughing, and said "it's safe to get out of your car. He's absolutely harmless. He just scares people."

My next surprise was when we entered his study, where I turned over the Air Force nuclear freeze materials I had put together for him. Next to his desk was a stack of books sitting on the floor. I don't remember the exact number, but there must have been about a dozen, stacked one on top of the other, with his academy award statue sitting on top of the books. It was at once disarming and extremely impressive to see the award displayed so simply. In many ways, Heston appeared to be a "down to earth" kind of guy.

On another date my wife and I escorted Charlton Heston at an Air Force Conference, which if memory serves me right, was held in the ballroom of the Century Plaza Hotel in Century City. As we were about to enter an elevator to take us to a meeting room, two young women exited the elevator and spotted Heston. Their eyes stayed fixed on Heston as they turned to walk away and I said to Heston: "I think you just got swooned by those two young ladies." In his charming way, he responded: "It all counts. I love my fans!"

In addition to supporting Charlton Heston in his debates, I wrote a lengthy feature article opposing the nuclear freeze that was cleared by the Department of Defense Office of Security Review and appeared in the *Journal of Defense & Diplomacy* and another article titled "Defense: Forget the Myths" that appeared in *The San Diego Union*. Between 1982 and 1984 I also wrote a series of letters to the editor opposing the nuclear freeze. They appeared in a variety of daily newspapers, including the *Los Angeles Times*.

One of the more interesting things I did while I was in Los Angeles was to write a speech on the nuclear freeze issue. During the 1980s the Arms Control Association pointed out that the Nuclear Weapons Freeze Campaign started by Randall Forsbert, a young defense and disarmament researcher, was designed to stop the drift toward nuclear war.

The freeze campaign escalated into a mass movement that swept across the United States. It attracted the support of nearly all peace groups, as well as that of mainstream religious, professional, and labor organizations. The nuclear freeze debates between Heston and Newman were just a symptom of the movement.

During the period I was supporting Heston while he was debating that subject with Newman I tried repeatedly to get a senior Air Force officer to address the subject. I had received what I thought were important public requests for an Air Force officer to give a presentation on that topic, but it was a very sensitive subject and I couldn't get anyone to address it publicly.

I wrote a nuclear freeze speech and got it cleared through the Department of Defense Security Review Office, after which I accepted a commitment to speak on the subject in front of the California Teachers Association in Los Angeles. I knew the majority of the teachers supported Newman's position on the subject and feared I might be confronted by a large group of angry teachers when they heard my speech.

Nevertheless, I thought it would be a great public forum and looked forward to meeting with them. They surprised me. There were hundreds of teachers in the room and while the pitch I presented was the exact opposite of the position they supported, they were very respectful, asked a lot of excellent questions, and thanked me for taking the time to visit with them. There was not the first hint of animosity or antagonism displayed. They seemed genuinely glad that I had taken the time to share the Air Force position on the nuclear freeze issue with them.

I was also treated well by the reporters who covered the speech. That particularly surprised me because they seemed predisposed toward Paul Newman's position on the nuclear freeze issue.

By the end of my time in Los Angeles the movement had dissipated quite a bit, especially during Ronald Reagan's presidency.

Over the course of three years in the Los Angeles office a major part of my job was to function as the Air Force technical advisor to the motion picture and television industry. Representatives of both industries frequently wanted to film on an Air Force base, which was by far cheaper for them than to build a replica of an Air Force base on a sound stage.

Technical Advisor to the Motion Picture and Television Industries

The Air Force would only support movie and television efforts if the theatrical productions depicted the Air Force in a responsible business-like setting fulfilling its missions in a professional way. Before I could offer our support to those industries, it was my job to read the scripts to make sure the movie and television executives were committed to depicting the Air Force professionally, without disparaging the Air Force through settings, dress, conduct or dialogue.

I also functioned as a liaison between the movie and television industries and the Department of Defense Security Review process, which meant making sure there was nothing classified in the scripts. Sometimes a scriptwriter would unintentionally and unknowingly include a description of Air Force equipment or situations that were classified, and I would have to excise that material and help the scriptwriter create an unclassified version before the scenes could be filmed.

Other than making sure the scripts were acceptable to the Air Force it was also my responsibility to make sure actors were dressed in the proper Air Force uniforms and otherwise acted in ways that accurately reflected conduct that was acceptable to the Air Force. That meant no sloppy salutes or slouched or unmilitary postures and no profane or unprofessional dialogue.

Over the course of the three years I was assigned to this office one of my representatives or I supported a legion of movie and television projects. I or a representative from my office served as the technical advisor for the movies *Megaforce, Firefox,* and *The Right Stuff,* and I helped create the movie and television series *Call to Glory.*

In the process of supporting *Call to Glory* the producers (Jonathan Avnet and Steve Tisch) and the writer (Ronald M. Cohen) pitched a plot that involved a classified aircraft and mission that was classified and simply had no chance of getting Air Force approval. So, I worked with them to help create a script that would be acceptable to the Air Force. It turned into *Call to Glory*, which was a successful movie-of-the week and an ABC-TV television series that was filmed at Paramount Studios and lasted for a year. I worked the movie and the first six episodes of *Call to Glory* before I retired.

My support included arranging for the scriptwriter to interview General Curtis LeMay who had served as the commander of the Strategic Air Command from 1948 to 1957 and who was probably the most knowledgeable person to interview about strategic aspects of the Air Force. Several Air Force friends had warned me that General LeMay might be difficult to work with because he was highly opinionated and dogmatic. It turned out he was a delight to work with. He was very pleased to see a movie and television program being developed that would showcase the Air Force and he was very cooperative with both the scriptwriter and me. Unfortunately, General LeMay died four years after *Call to Glory* was made into a movie-of-the-week.

The movie, *Call to Glory*, which followed the 1984 Olympics, related to the U-2 flights over Cuba during the 1962 Cuban Missile Crisis while Colonel Raynor Sarnac, a fictional character, was stationed at Edwards AFB, California during the 1960s. The movie was heavy on the drama of the Cuban missile crisis; however, during the production run of the television series, the show came to focus more on the loneliness experienced by wife Vanessa Sarnac (Cindy Pickett)) while stationed on base, and what she and the family would do to spend time in productive pursuits while enduring the Antelope Valley's then more noticeable isolation from civilization. In short, it was a movie that focused on the daily routines of an Air Force family.

In addition to Craig T. Nelson as Colonel Sarnac (the lead character) , the cast included Keenan Wynn, Cindy Pickett, and Elisabeth Shue, as well as David Hollander, Gabriel Damon, Thomas O'Brien, and David Lain Baker. Incidentally, Elisabeth Shue, who was 20-years-old at that time, but looked about 16, preferred to be known as Lisa Shue and some years later she was a very successful member of the "CSI" television series cast. "CSI" was cancelled after 15 years on the air.

The *Call to Glory* cast was a joy to work with. None of them had what some might call a "big head." They were all down to earth and available to me any time I needed to advise them on a matter of Air Force concern about the show. As a sign of his commitment to the role of Colonel Sarnac, during the break between filming the movie of the week and filming the first episodes of the television series Craig T. Nelson went on a diet and lost about 30 pounds so he could really look the part of an Air Force colonel.

Also, to help Nelson get into his role, he was given familiarization rides in USAF T-38, the F-4 Phantom II, and the F-16 Fighting Falcon aircraft at Edwards Air Force Base during the filming of the series.

Call to Glory was initially very popular and very successful. Since it followed the telecast of the 1984 Summer Olympics, it was an immediate ratings success at the outset, but with the success of the series, ABC decided to move away from the historical aspects of the show to concentrate on more "soap opera" situations with the Sarnac family, which resulted in a severe viewer drop-off, and the show was cancelled after one season. But back then a season ran 22 episodes; today a season only runs 13 episodes.

When I retired from the Air Force I received nice letters from the cast thanking me for my support. One letter was especially touching. Keenan Wynn wrote such a sentimental letter you would have thought he knew me for 20 years. I cherish it because he died shortly after the series ended.

There were other Air Force projects my staff and I supported throughout the three years I directed this office of talented and skilled people, far too many to include here. It was an exciting period in my life and over the three years, I worked with an incredible array of talented celebrities, including Barry Bostick, Buster Crabbe, Charlton Heston, Clint Eastwood, Dennis Weaver, Henry Silva, James B. Sikking, James Shigeta, Jimmy Stewart, John Denver, Lorne Green, Morgan Woodward, Nick Nolte, Ricardo Montalban, and Wilfred Hyde-White. There were many, many more, but you get the picture.

However, I do want to make special mention of one actor, James Shigeta About every three months I would put together a group of civic leaders and entertainment celebrities to take on a tour of NORAD and the Air Force Academy. Occasionally I would also take a group on a tour of the Strategic Air Command. We would load them on one of our aircraft and take them to Colorado Springs or to Offutt Air Force Base, Nebraska, where we would take them on a tour of these famous military facilities.

Some of the entertainers wanted to explore downtown, which generally meant they wanted to bar-hop. I never participated or told them where to go; I simply explained that was not part of the tour and turned them loose. However, their downtown excursions never created any problems for the Air Force.

James Shigeta was different; he was the epitome of a family man. All he wanted to know was where he could get tee-shirts with NORAD or the Air Force Academy on them to give to his kids. He was incredibly proud of his family and wanted to take home a souvenir for his kids. What was just as interesting to me was the really nice "thank you" note he sent to me after the tour. We exchanged Christmas cards every year afterwards for the rest of his life. He died in 2016. He was one of the most genuinely good people I met in the entertainment industry, and he was one of their very best representatives. He was a genuine gentleman, in the original meaning of that term.

I experienced similar situations with other celebrities in Los Angeles, but this book isn't about celebrities, and I don't want to risk embarrassing any of them by mentioning them by name. I'm confident James Shigeta and Charlton Heston would not mind me mentioning these experiences. They were warm and wonderful guys.

Of all the celebrities I met during my three years in Hollywood, the person I was most excited to meet was General Jimmy Doolittle, the famous Army Air Force pilot who led 16 B-25s on a raid of Tokyo on April 18, 1942. It was the first air strike of the Japanese home islands after the Japanese attack on Pearl Harbor on Sunday, December 7, 1941. The raid caused negligible material damage to Japan, but it achieved its goal of raising American morale and casting doubt in Japan on the ability of its military leaders to defend their home islands. Peggy and I met general Doolittle in 1984 at an Air Force conference in Los Angeles. When I met him he was gracious and posed for a photo with my wife and me. Regrettably he died in 1993.

During my 30-year military career, in addition to service and campaign ribbons, I was awarded the Legion of Merit (which is generally reserved for colonels and general officers), the Meritorious Service Medal, the Joint Service Commendation Medal, and two Air Force Commendation Medals. Not bad for a small town Irish lad from southern Illinois.

In 1984 I decided it was time to retire from the military and move on to a new career. I had spent 30 years in an unusual combination of service: eight years enlisted in the Navy, 22 years commissioned in the Air Force, and seven of those 22 years I worked in joint assignments with the Army. So, I had literally spent a bit of time with each of our three major branches of service. But I felt it was time to retire.

Some friends had already retired from the Air Force and were working in various positions for different corporations, so I circulated word that I was ready to retire from the Air Force and would be interested in using my considerable public affairs experiences in the corporate world. Within a short time I had a nibble from the LTV Aerospace and Defense Company's AM General Division, located in Detroit, Michigan.

CHAPTER 6
AN EXCITING LIFE IN THE CIVILIAN WORLD

After spending 30 years in the military I looked forward to starting a civilian career. I didn't have to wait long! A friend of mine, who was working in Dallas for a national company, knew that LTV Aerospace and Defense Company was looking for someone to start a new public affairs department at one of its divisions located in the Detroit area.

He told the company about my public relations background and my impending retirement from the Air Force, and they contacted me to see if my public relations background was compatible with LTV's interests and needs and to see if I would be interested in moving to Michigan to create a new department in one of their divisions.

With about 25 years of public affairs experience, an undergraduate degree in communications, and a graduate degree in public relations, and with 10 hours towards a doctorate, the leadership of LTV's AM General Division was confident I had the requisite credentials to start a public affairs department in a division that had never had a public affairs or communications program. It was an opportunity to start from scratch with a reputable and credible defense contractor that, incidentally, offered me an attractive salary that could complement my Air Force retirement income. So I accepted the position, retired from the Air Force and Peggy and I drove straight to Michigan, without stopping anywhere enroute to Detroit.

That was a big mistake for me personally. My wife complained that we missed a lot of tourist sites along the way to Detroit—that we may never have a chance to visit again. I should have taken a couple of days to play tourist. Even 33 years later she occasionally reminds me that we sure missed an opportunity to visit a lot of great sights.

AM General LLC

AM General LLC traces its beginnings to the Standard Wheel Company of Terre Haute, Indiana, in 1903. It eventually became the Kaiser Jeep Corporation, which was later purchased by American Motors Corporation (AMC). AMC then changed the Kaiser Jeep Corporation name to AM General, and it was later sold to LTV Aerospace and Defense Company. LTV changed the name of its new division to AM General Division. In 1992 LTV Aerospace and Defense Company sold its AM General Division to the Renco Group and AM General became AM General LLC, which then became, and is now, an independent company.

At the point I joined AM General it had an illustrious history as a company that had built over 150,000 U.S. Postal Service "dispatcher" vehicles for the Post Office, police departments, utility companies, and small package delivery firms. It was also a respected defense contractor that had built 150,000 2-1/2–ton and 112,000 5-ton trucks for armed forces around the world. Its sterling reputation was an advantage to LTV Aerospace and Defense as it continued to expand its defense business.

In 1983 AM General had won an Army contract valued at $1.2 billion to build 55,000 High Mobility Multi-purpose Wheeled Vehicles (HMMWV) over a five year period. When I joined the company in 1984 it was just beginning to build the HMMWVs in its assembly plant located in Mishawaka, Indiana, a city with a population of about 48,000.

Mishawaka was a bit over five miles from South Bend, Indiana. At that time AM General was in the process of moving its corporate headquarters from the American Motors property in Detroit to a new location in Livonia, Michigan, as a new division of LTV Aerospace and Defense Company.

Shortly after I was hired I learned that LTV intended to move the AM General Division headquarters to its South Bend, Indiana facilities, which incidentally was where the company continued to built its 2-1/2 ton and 5-ton trucks. We would be headquartered in South Bend, Indiana, although our HMMWV assembly plant, which was the single-most important AM General product, was located in Mishawaka.

For those of you who aren't familiar with the HMMWV, it is the Army's replacement for its ubiquitous M151 utility vehicle, known more popularly as the "jeep." The HMMWV was known variously as a HMMWV, Humvee, or

Hummer (manufacturer's registered trademark name for its commercial versions). Initially AM General had named the HMMWV the "Hummer," but that name did not catch on with the U.S. Army, which liked to establish its own name for its equipment. Consequently, AM General agreed to call the vehicle a HMMWV, but several years later AM General designated "Hummer" as the name for its commercial version of this unique vehicle.

The commercial version of the Hummer is a separate story that was not part of my time at AM General. All the while I served with the AM General Division, nobody at the division or at the parent company believed there would ever be any interest in a commercial version of the military's off-road vehicle. They were wrong. It turned out much later that there was a considerable commercial market for the civilian version of the military's HMMWV.

The HMMWV is a rugged off-road vehicle that has a ground clearance of 16 inches. That much ground clearance makes it possible for the HMMWV to navigate over virtually any terrain and overcome seemingly impossible obstacles. It is a technologically advanced 1-1/4-ton, 4x4, multipurpose vehicle that almost instantly became a legend in the field, rivaling the "jeep's" popularity with soldiers.

In 1984 Jeffrey C. Wright, AM General's senior vice-president, worldwide marketing and strategic planning, described the HMMWV as "one of Army's most successful truck acquisitions." It replaced a medley of vehicles, including some M151s, all M274s (1/4-ton Mule), all M561s (1-1/2-ton Gama Goat), and some M880s (1-1/4-ton pick-trucks). As I would point out to reporters during my tenure with this company, the HMMWV became the most versatile vehicle introduced to the Army since soldiers stepped down off of horses, even more versatile than the ubiquitous "jeep."

The HMMWV was, and still is, a powerful, very mobile and versatile centerpiece of the U.S. Army's wheeled vehicle force modernization program. It was manufactured in different configurations (cargo/troop carriers, weapons carriers, ambulances, and communications carriers), all with the same chassis and power train. Eventually it came in 20 configurations, including an up-armored, expanded capacity vehicle and international variants. It had a curb weight of 5,100 lbs. A 150-horsepower, 6.2-liter, V-8 diesel engine provided its power, with a 25-gallon fuel tank, which gave the HUMVEE speed, agility and range. A 6.5-liter, 170-horsepower engine powered a later version, which had a naturally aspirated, fuel-injected General Motors V-8 diesel engine, and an electronically controlled four-speed automatic transmission, four-wheel power disc brakes, and power-assisted steering.

Unlike any other wheeled vehicle, HUMVEES then and now can scale 18-inch vertical walls, climb 60% grades, traverse 40% slide-slopes, overcome moguls, muscle through deep sand and mud, ford two feet of water, plow through three-foot snowdrifts, and navigate virtually any terrain, while carrying up to 1-1/4-tons of people and cargo. Upgraded versions can carry up to two tons. They can also run about 30 miles on run-flat tires, which would be a huge benefit to soldiers in combat if the tires were shot. Without the run-flat capability a soldier with a disabled vehicle would be stranded and subject to increased enemy threat. The run-flat capability gave the vehicle great versatility.

When I arrived at AM General, the HMMWV was not yet widely known, despite the fact that the U.S. Army circulated a news release in 1983 announcing its addition to the Army's fleet of vehicles. I was hired to establish a public relations department and was given the title of director of public relations and advertising. The first thing I did was to establish a department that consisted of two secretaries, a public affairs specialist and me. Next, after establishing the company's first ever pubic relations department, I established a public relations and advertising plan that included as its objective:

"To support our domestic and international marketing efforts; to increase public awareness of our products; to build on our established community relations in Indiana; to foster better employee communications; and to support LTV Corporate public relations programs."

The next thing on my agenda, after establishing the public relations plan, was to introduce myself to the local news media outlets, both print and broadcast, as well as regional and national media outlets that focused exclusively on defense matters. Reporters were particularly happy about my assignment because they often had questions that couldn't be answered because of the unavailability of an AM General division spokesman.

In the summer of 1984, as part of an international introduction of the HMMWV, we put the HMMWV on display for a week at the Farnborough International Air Show, just outside London, England. The Farnborough International Airshow is a weeklong event that combines a major trade exhibition for the aerospace and defense industries with a public air show. The event is held in mid-July in even-numbered years at the Farnborough Airport in Hampshire.

The first four days are dedicated exclusively to trade, while the final three days are open to the public.

With over 1,500 exhibitors, 80,000 square meters of exhibition space, a static aircraft park and flying display, and over 70,000 visitors during the trade days alone, it was an ideal opportunity to introduce the HMMWV to an international audience. The connection of our vehicle to the air show was that it could be used for airport perimeter defense.

The Farnborough International Air Show attracts major news media coverage, and we were able to generate a lot of excellent international coverage of our newest off-road vehicle. It was also my first opportunity to introduce myself to international reporters who covered the European defense circuit. That proved to be very valuable because many, if not most, of the international reporters also covered defense related matters in the United States, and I would later be able to cement my relations with them at international shows and exhibits in the United States.

The next project was to participate in the annual defense exhibition in September 1984 at the Sheraton Hotel, located in Washington, DC. AM General displayed a version of the HMMWV, and I worked with the division marketing vice president and his staff to garner as much public and news media exposure as we could generate on our newest replacement for the "jeep." Jeffrey Wright, vice president of marketing, integrated me into his expanded marketing effort and we worked closely together sharing information with the international news media.

The annual defense exhibition attracts national and international defense organizations that display their wares for a week. Like the Farnborough International Air Show, the annual defense exhibition at the Sheraton Hotel attracts news media representatives from around the world who report on the latest defense equipment. The result of our first national exhibition with the HMMWV was a great deal of coverage, especially in Washington, DC-based publications.

The problem was that these reporters were not able to report on our vehicle from a personal perspective from driving the vehicle in the kind of environments for which it was designed to be driven. So our next public relations effort was intended to generate maximum exposure by providing reporters with just such an experience.

We took several HMMWVs to Jean Dry Lake, about 30 miles east of Carson

City, Nevada, which offered an ideal off-road environment in which reporters could experience driving the HMMWVs in the kind of off-road environment that would showcase its capabilities and provide them with first-hand experiences they could relate to in the articles they filed for their publications, radio and television stations, or both.

We invited about 30 print and broadcast reporters from across America, including representatives from major news media outlets from both coasts, as well as international reporters who specialized in reporting on defense- oriented vehicles, to attend our "ride and drive" program. It was the kind of opportunity many of the reporters had been requesting ever since the HMMWV first hit the streets.

Jean Dry Lake includes some of the most desolate, rocky and sandy areas in North America, all of which would be ideal for demonstrating how well our unique off-road HMMWV could handle difficult terrain. To give the reporters the best option for reporting on the performance of these wonderful vehicles, we briefed them on the HMMWV's capabilities and safety issues, then we let them test drive the vehicles without any interference from us. It was an ideal way for the reporters to get a valuable hands-on experience as a user of the advanced technology these vehicles represented.

The first-hand driving experience for these reporters resulted in massive positive media coverage throughout the United States. As an unintended and surprising result of the positive coverage, HMMWVs also began appearing in major action-oriented motion pictures. More and more of our "jeep" replacements entered the military inventory, and its members became increasingly familiar with and supportive of it, so more of the HMMWVs began showing up in movies depicting the military.

The part I enjoyed the most was not meeting all of the important international reporters; it was the food in Carson City, Nevada. Over the week we were at Jean Dry Lake we returned to town every evening and searched out popular restaurants. Without mentioning any names I can tell you Carson City has outstanding restaurants that serve the largest, juiciest, best tasting steaks I've ever eaten anywhere in the world. It is worth a trip to Carson City, Nevada just to eat their steaks.

Recognizing that not all reporters could attend our ride-and-drive at Jean Dry Lake, we continued to invite those who could make it to come to our South Bend,

Indiana manufacturing facility where we would encourage them to drive the vehicles on our company property. It wasn't as good as the wonderful terrain at Jean Dry Lake, but it still resulted in positive articles being written about the HMMWV.

To make sure the Department of Defense knew about the rapidly expanding HMWWV reputation, I coordinated with our general manager and invited Deputy Secretary of Defense William Howard Taft IV to visit and tour our HMMWV manufacturing and assembly plant. He accepted our invitation and the visit was scheduled.

In between the time we invited Secretary Taft to visit our facilities and his scheduled visit, our general manager retired and a new general manager was named. When he heard that we had invited the Deputy Secretary of Defense to visit the manufacturing and assembly plant, he called me into his office and told me it was "the stupidest" thing he had ever heard of because we would almost certainly have to close down production while the Secretary was touring the plant to speak with employees.

The new general manager then angrily acknowledged that it was too late to cancel the visit, so we would just have to live with the stupid decision. But he advised me to never again schedule a public relations event that would require us to shut down our production and assembly line.

Secretary Taft's visit went exceptionally well and everyone from AM General through the Army's chain of command was very happy with the visit. It was a major news story and we got a lot of publicity out of it, including front-page photos of the Deputy Secretary of Defense driving a HMMWV off our assembly line. Equally as important, we established a lot of good will with our Army and Defense Department customer base—good will that we would not otherwise have had.

As a consequence, the day after the Secretary's visit I was called back into the general manger's office and he marveled at what a wonderful idea it was to have invited the Deputy Secretary of Defense to visit our plant. He acknowledged that the temporary shutdown of our assembly line was insignificant, and the long-term benefits of his visit would undoubtedly be monumental. There was not the slightest mention of the severe criticism he had previously given me for orchestrating the Secretary's visit.

I continued to generate as much news media and public attention to our vehicle as I could during the next few months. Meanwhile, unbeknown to me, the AM General vice-president of marketing, who owned a home in the Detroit area, was impressed with my performance at AM General and had discussed my performance with one of his friends, who was the general manager of General Dynamics Land Systems (GDLS), a division of the General Dynamics Corporation that was building the Army's Abrams Main Battle Tank. Our vice-president of marketing knew I was not happy with our new general manager, so he felt free to discuss my AM General performance with his friend.

The next thing I knew I was contacted by the vice-president of human resources for GDLS about the possibility that I might consider starting a public affairs department at his location in Sterling Heights, Michigan. I was very interested, so we quietly arranged for me to visit the GDLS headquarters to discuss the options.

The interviews with the vice-president of human resources and the general manager went very well, lasting for several hours, and within a few days the GDLS general manager and vice-president of human resources together contacted me and offered me a position. They wanted me to establish a public affairs department at their Sterling Heights headquarters. I accepted their generous offer and scheduled my start there after a two-week notice to AM General.

I next wrote a resignation letter and presented it to the new general manager of AM General and notified him that I would be leaving in two weeks to go to work for the General Dynamics Corporation. He was shocked and just about fell out of his chair. I explained that after working with him for a few months I had become convinced that he and I would never see the pubic affairs function in the same way and that he would be better off having someone with whom he was more comfortable having work for him.

Even though he and LTV Aerospace and Defense Company officials, tried to talk me into staying at AM General, I politely said my goodbyes to everyone concerned and made arrangements to move to Michigan and begin work at GDLS. I didn't discover until I was on station at my new job that several other AM General marketing people had also interviewed for the job. However, none of them had the kind of dependable public relations or marketing background that General Dynamics Land Systems was looking for.

Before I departed AM General I recommended several potential and very qualified people to be considered to fill my position, one of whom was an active duty Army public affairs officer. As it turned out the former Department of the Army public affairs officer whom I had known for several years while working in the Pentagon and with whom I had often worked through the years was selected to be my replacement. Because of his availability there was very little public relations down time for AM General.

I was glad I was able to start a new assignment with another company without leaving my previous company in a delicate position without a qualified public relations and advertising representative to look after their interests. I was mindful that no employee should ever burn bridges during a career progression, so despite my brief spat with the general manager, I left AM General feeling like I was fair with them.

General Dynamics Land Systems Division (GDLS)

GDLS is a division of the General Dynamics Corporation. The General Dynamics corporate headquarters is located in Falls Church, Virginia, with four subordinate groups: the Aerospace Group, which focuses on superior aircraft design; the Combat Systems Group, which is a global leader in tracked and wheeled military vehicles, weapons systems, and munitions; the Information Systems and Technology Group, which provides technologies, products, and services that address a range of secure mobile communication systems; and the Marine Systems Group, which designs, builds, and supports submarines and surface ships for the U.S. Navy.

GDLS was the division of General Dynamics Corporation that was building the Abrams Main Battle Tank (MBT) when I was hired. It was formerly known as Chrysler Defense until 1982 when General Dynamics Corporation bought it for $336.1 million. It was then renamed General Dynamics Land Systems Division,

GDLS also operates the Lima Army Tank Plant in Lima, Ohio, the General Dynamics Anniston Operations in Anniston, Alabama, and two smaller operations located in Tallahassee, Florida, and Scranton, Pennsylvania. It is still known as GDLS and its headquarters is still located in Sterling Heights, Michigan.

Today GDLS is an American manufacturer of military vehicles, such as main battle tanks and lighter armored fighting vehicles. It also has a Canadian subsidiary, known as GDLS-C, that is a major supplier of armored vehicles of all types, including the LAV-25, the Stryker, and variety of lightly armored vehicles that are all based on the same chassis as the Lightly Armored Vehicles (LAV) and Stryker vehicles.

I was hired to create a public affairs department. The main GDLS product was the Abrams Main Battle Tank, which was named after deceased Army General Creighton Abrams. My title was going to be director of communications, which was considered to be all-inclusive and would include more communications than public relations and advertising.

I established a new department with one other public affairs specialist and two secretaries, all of who were fairly long-term GDLS employees and all of who were happy to be assigned to a new communications department. They had been advised of the functional nature of our new department before accepting their new assignments.

I was also very surprised and quite excited by the fact that the vice-president of personnel had placed me in a vice-president's office where I would spend the rest of my time at GDLS. It was quite unusual because while GDLS had a large number of directors, I was the only one who was treated to a protocol that was generally only extended to vice-presidents. I would discover that as a member of the general manager's staff reporting directly to him, I tended to be treated as a vice-president by other members of his staff and generally by everyone else at GDLS. It was a welcome privilege I had not expected.

One of my initial goals at GDLS was to establish myself as the division contact for the news media and community leaders. I sent out a memo to members of the local news media including the *Detroit Free Press*, the *Detroit News, The Macomb Daily* (county newspaper), *The Source* (Sterling Heights newspaper), as well as the network-affiliated television stations. I then contacted the local Chambers of Commerce and identified myself as their new point of contact as the GDLS director of communications.

Shortly after my introduction to the community leaders, I was invited to serve on the Sterling Heights, Michigan Chamber of Commerce and the Warren, Michigan Chamber of Commerce. Of course I accepted and served on both for the duration of my time at GDLS. Through the Chambers of Commerce we developed a robust community relations program

Abrams Main Battle Tank

As I had previously done after establishing a new public relations and advertising department at AM General LLC, one of the first things I did after establishing my new department at GDLS was to contact my extensive list of news media contacts around the world and let them know about my new position with the General Dynamics Corporation.

I wanted them to know that I would be their principal contact for information about a corporate perspective on the Army's Abrams Main Battle Tank. They could still rely on their Army public affairs contacts in the Pentagon for a specific Army perspective on this centerpiece of its land forces, but I was going to be their single contact for the contractor's perspective.

I then made repeated visits to our Lima Army Tank Plant, where the main battle tanks were manufactured and assembled, to familiarize myself with the leadership and briefers responsible for tank onsite production. The Lima Army Tank Plant was a GOCO (government owned, contractor operated) operation that included GDLS leaders as well as Army leaders and briefers.

Since I would frequently be escorting news media reporters through the tank plant for general orientation and specific briefings, I needed to become knowledgeable about tank production and to personally know the plant managers and briefers. I had to do the same at our Tallahassee, Florida, and Scranton, Pennsylvania, facilities where many of the vital parts for the tanks are manufactured.

Part of my job was to make sure the general public and especially the international news media knew that an investment in main battle tank production is an essential investment in one of America's vital national resources.

For instance, international customers who buy Abrams MBTs benefit from an extensive research and development program in which the U.S. Army invests millions of dollars each year to insure that its MBTs reflect the latest technological advancements. Those advancements are reflected in the successful historical lineage of M1 Series MBTs. Continuous R&D investments by the U.S. government paid handsome dividends on the battlefield during the Gulf War of 1991, during which Abrams tanks devastated Soviet-built Iraqi tanks without losing a single American tank in the process.

The bottom line is this. Production of the Abrams MBT provides soldiers with a technological edge on the battlefield, establishes long-term job skills for the public and private sector industries, and stimulates a serious boost to the overall United States economy.

In 1988 during the United States presidential election competition I had an opportunity to showcase the Abrams MBT in a uniquely extraordinary way. During the run-up to the election between Vice President George H.W. Bush and Governor Michael Dukakis, the Dukakis campaign had scheduled a stop in the Detroit area. Knowing that they would be in our area, I contacted the Dukakis campaign headquarters and offered their candidate an orientation ride in the Abrams MBT at our headquarters in Sterling Heights. It would offer them a unique opportunity to attract a lot of news media coverage of their candidate riding in our tank and form a backdrop for him to tout his national defense perspective.

We had earlier offered the same opportunity to Vice President Bush, who declined our offer. However, the Dukakis campaign jumped at the opportunity and we scheduled the visit for September 13, 1988. On the day of the event, we were flooded with national news media, both those who were accompanying Governor Dukakis, as well as local reporters, and we had set up bleachers and stands for the general public, GDLS employees, and front-row seats for the news media.

Our vice president of engineering, who pointed out that there is nothing soft in the tank, gave Governor Dukakis a safety briefing. Dukakis was told the tank is made almost entirely of steel, and if he bumped his head on anything it could be very painful, which is why we require anyone who rides in our tanks to wear a helmet. Once suited up for the orientation ride in front of a huge crowd, he was placed in the tank in which he was allowed to stand up looking out of a crew hatch and the ride began.

His campaign people considered the orientation ride to be a key image of his campaign that might help him overcome his perceived softness on defense issues. The tank approached the stands at a reasonably high speed and then came to a sudden stop in front of the stands so news media photographers could get some great shots of Dukakis in the tank.

For several days after the event everyone seemed to think Dukakis had scored a huge coup over Bush. Then news stories began to appear all over the country with photos showing the helmeted Dukakis standing in the tank, and news stories were not complimentary about that vision. Instead, it turned into a huge disappointment for him and his staff when reporters said it made him look even softer on defense.

Politico Magazine carried the headline "Dukakis and the Tank, The inside story of the worst campaign photo op ever." It went on to say:

"Matt Bennett can still hear the reporters laughing, all 90 of them. He can still picture Sam Donaldson doubled over, guffawing, on a riser that looked out over a dusty field in suburban Detroit. The visit, meant to bolster the candidate's credibility as a future commander-in-chief, would go down as one of the worst campaign backfires in history."

·   ·   ·

Bennett was a 23-year-old political rookie in 1988 when he was sent to our facility to organize a campaign stop for Dukakis.

Critical comments appeared in newspapers and magazines all over the country and what was supposed to be a great political photo op for the Governor turned into his worst nightmare. As an aside, the Dukakis campaign people had promised if I sent some photos to them, the Governor would inscribe them for us to hand out to our employees. After the tank ride I sent a pile of photos to them but never heard back from anyone.

The event worked well for us, not so much for the Dukakis campaign. The reason we arranged for Governor Dukakis to ride in the tank was to garner positive exposure for the tank, which it did. Nowhere in any of the news stories in either print or broadcast media coverage was a single disparaging word mentioned about the Abrams MBT. In fact, we received massive positive coverage of the tank. So, while the event failed for Governor Dukakis, it worked out wonderfully well for General Dynamics Corporation.

What I hadn't anticipated was the fallout for me. For months whenever I went out into the community to give talks about our MBTs, I was introduced as the guy who put Dukakis in the tank, which destroyed his run for president. I didn't put him in the tank literally, I only arranged for the event. Gordon England, our vice president of engineering actually put him into the tank. Even so, I always felt uneasy about that and thought it was necessary to explain to my audiences that we didn't schedule the MBT demonstration to benefit Governor Dukakis; we scheduled it so we could get as much positive coverage of the MBT as possible. It worked for us; it did not work for the Governor.

Later I made sure that my international news media contacts received the latest data on performance of the Abrams MBT during combat in the Middle East while performing in Operation Desert Storm. The Abrams MBT became known as "The Desert Storm Champion." Under the cover of darkness, 320 M1A1 Abrams MBTs dashed 200 kilometers across southern Iraqi without having a single breakdown; then engaged and destroyed the enemy without losing a single tank of its own in the battle. That's the kind of reliability Abrams tank crews depended on during the Gulf War in 1991. It is also part of the heritage that is the foundation for the U.S. Army's latest MBT, the M1A2.

In the armored vehicle world, the M1A2 is in a class by itself. While there are three or four excellent MBTs available on the international market, Abrams tanks are arguably the soldier's choice in a clash of armored technology on the battlefield. The M1A2 is an evolutionary leap forward from its predecessor, the M1A1, which performed so magnificently in Operation Desert Storm in 1991.

I explained to all of my news media contacts that no American soldiers died in Abrams MBTs as a result of enemy action in the Gulf War and enemy tanks did not destroy any Abrams tanks. Our Army and Marines using Abrams tanks dominated the battlefield.

I was always proud to tell reporters that weapons become obsolete almost as fast as they come off the drawing board. A nation that falls behind technologically is immediately at a disadvantage on the battlefield. I pointed out that Iraqi forces had a dramatic numerical edge in men and armored equipment, but they were no match for the superior technology of the Abrams MBTs.

According to an article, *The Abrams Tank Next Generation*, by Joel Baglole, dated December 26, 2017, "The U.S. Army deployed its next generation Abrams tank – known as the M1A3 – in combat in 2017. Army officials have said they plan to keep the latest iteration of the long-serving tank in service until 2050.

The M1A3 Abrams is outfitted with a number of enhancements over previous versions of the tank. To make it lighter and more mobile, the Army replaced the M256 smoothbore gun with a lighter 120-millimeter cannon; added road wheels and an improved suspension system; installed a more durable track; used lighter armor; and inserted precision armaments capable of hitting targets from 12 kilometers. Plans also call for the addition of an infrared camera and laser detector.

In keeping with previous improvements in the evolution of the Abrams tanks, these upgrades will make the Abrams main battle tank more effective on the battlefield.

Stryker Lightly Armored Vehicle

Another vehicle I was proud to discuss publicly was the Stryker vehicle, which was being developed as my tour with GDLS was coming to a close in 1993. The Stryker, which is now in full production, has been fielded and serves in the U.S. Army, is a lightly armored family of eight-wheeled vehicles produced by General Dynamics Land Systems Canada in London, Ontario, Canada.

The Stryker is a family of eight-wheeled armored fighting vehicles derived from the Canadian LAV III and based on the Swiss Piranha III 8x8. Stryker vehicles have 4-wheel drive (8×4), but can be switched to all-wheel drive (8×8). According to GDLS the vehicle comes in several variants with a common engine, transmission, hydraulics, wheels, tires, differentials and transfer case. The M1130 Command Vehicle and M1133 Medical Evacuation vehicle have an air conditioning unit mounted on the back. The medical vehicle also has a higher-capacity generator. A recent upgrade program provided a field retrofit kit to add air conditioning units to all variants, and production started in 2005 on the Mobile Gun System mounting an overhead GDLS 105 mm automatic gun.

The Stryker's hull is constructed from high-hardness steel, which offers a basic level of protection against 14.5 mm rounds on the frontal arc, and all-around protection against 7.62 mm ball ammunition. In addition to this, Strykers are also equipped with bolt-on ceramic armor which offers all-around protection against 14.5 mm, armor-piercing ammunition, and artillery fragments from 155 mm rounds.

With the exception of some specialized variants, the primary armament of the Stryker is a Protector M151 Remote Weapon Station with .50-cal M2 machine gun, 7.62 mm M240 machine gun, or Mk 19 automatic grenade launcher.

According to *HomeofHeroes.com*, the Stryker was named after two unrelated soldiers separated by a generation, both of whom had been posthumously awarded our nation's highest award, the Medal of Honor: Pfc. Stuart S. Stryker, who died heroically in World War II and Spc. Robert F. Stryker, who died heroically fighting in South Vietnam.

GDLS claims its vehicles are the symbol of protection, the symbol of strength, and the symbol of innovation. "When our military receives a Stryker or any of our specialty wheeled vehicles...it knows it's getting the best equipment and the most advanced technology in the world.

Failing Health

In 1989, I almost died from a major heart attack. I was getting major chest pains when I walked with my wife for exercise. I thought I was having some kind of lung trouble, so I went to see my family doctor to find out what might cause the pains. She suspected the cause was my heart, not my lungs.

A cardiologist checked me out and also suspected the heart as a cause of the pains, so he scheduled a cardiac catheterization. During the cardiac catheterization he discovered that my circumflex artery, which feeds blood to the back side of the heart, was 80% blocked. Others were partially blocked but not as significantly as the circumflex artery.

So, my cardiologist did a balloon angioplasty to inflate and open the artery. It seemed to work well, after which I rested for a few hours and ate lunch. Unfortunately, there were no stents in those days (1989). He opened the artery and hoped (prayed) it would stay open.

After lunch, my cardiologist removed the shunt from my groin and prepared me for recovery in another part of the hospital. When he removed the shunt, my circumflex artery collapsed and shut off the flow of blood, causing a massive heart attack. I immediately went from having one cardiologist working on me, to having about six doctors working on me.

After nearly dying three times in about 15 minutes, I survived, but instead of being in the hospital for about two days I was in a recovery room for a week. The heart attack literally killed the bottom half of my heart and I have now survived for 28 years on half a heart. Good doctors and excellent medicine have kept me fairly healthy for all those years.

I occasionally still get chest pains (angina) when I do things too fast, but all I have to do is slow down when that happens and the pain subsides. I've been very fortunate to have good cardiologists taking care of me over the years, but I no longer take my good health for granted.

For awhile I thought I might have to retire from the General Dynamics

Corporation permanently because of my heart issue; however, after a three-month rest I recovered enough to return to work at General Dynamics Land Systems Division, where for four more years I continued to represent them as the director of communications for their public affairs department.

General Dynamics Corporation Headquarters

In the summer of 1993 I decided it was time for me to actually retire, so I notified my GDLS leadership and the corporate vice president of public affairs, and contacted our Human Resources director so I could process the necessary paperwork. However, while I was processing the retirement paperwork, the corporate vice president of public affairs asked if I would consider working at the corporate headquarters as his corporate director of public affairs for a period while he recruited a permanent replacement for that open position. The position had been open for a few months because the previous corporate director of public affairs had retired.

After discussing my options with my wife I agreed to delay my retirement for a period, while a suitable permanent replacement could be found. Meanwhile we had built a retirement home in Melbourne, Florida, and we decided my wife and mother, who had been living with us, would relocate to Florida while I continued on in Falls Church, Virginia, where the corporate headquarters was and still is located. The plan was for me to visit my family a couple of weekends during my stay at the corporate headquarters, and my wife would visit with me once or twice until I could join them in Melbourne sometime in mid-1994.

I rented an apartment in Falls Church, Virginia about two blocks from the corporate headquarters and began work as the new director of public affairs for General Dynamics Corporation. Not only did I get a new title, but it also came with a considerable pay raise and a potentially large bonus, which ultimately increased the sum of my monthly retirement check.

In November 1993 GDLS held a retirement party for me in Michigan that was attended by all of the corporate headquarters secretaries and a large number of corporate executives and specialists. It was a spectacular farewell dinner party during which an unbelievable number of vice presidents spoke glowingly about my value to the corporation and how much I would be missed. I also received a generous number of farewell gifts, including a professional golf bag, golf balls and tees, and a large cartoonish artwork of me in a golf cart, signed by even more people than those attending the party. Twenty-four years later it still hangs on the wall in my home study.

I went to the corporate headquarters expecting to stay only a couple of months while they recruited a suitable replacement; however, I spent eight months there, which made me think if I wanted to retire any time soon I would just have to leave them in a lurch. While it wasn't something I wanted to do, I was missing my wife and thought it was time to start my retirement.

I stayed at the corporate headquarters for a full eight months before actually retiring. During that time I was responsible for coordinating the division public affairs/communications programs and an internal corporate headquarters program I had not anticipated. Every morning I was expected to scan daily national newspapers and television news reports for corporate-or defense-related items of interest to our senior executives.

I scanned such newspapers as *The New York Times, Wall Street Journal, Washington Post,* and several others, clipping relevant news articles of interest to our leadership. I then pasted them together in a newsletter format, after which I reproduced them and distributed them throughout the corporate headquarters. Although time consuming, it was very interesting assignment because I was now concerned with products developed by all of the General Dynamics divisions instead of just GDLS.

The remainder of my time was devoted to news media relations since I was the corporate focal point for all news media inquiries worldwide. While I had always enjoyed good relations with my national and international news media contacts, the difference was that as the corporate public affairs officer I was expected to be knowledgeable about major programs at all of our divisions instead of just GDLS. That took a lot of study and a lot of close coordination with my contacts at each division, but I loved it. I was always excited to be able to represent our corporation publicly, whether with the general public or with the international news media, including those who focused exclusively on defense contractors.

Those reporters who focused mostly on defense contractors were always the most interesting because they were the most knowledgeable and asked the most intelligent questions. I knew a lot of them because for years I had participated in a large number of defense-oriented shows and exhibits, at which I had met most of the international reporters who attended those events.

To help pass the time while I was living alone in Falls Church, I would get up early, like 5:00 a.m., dress and go for a two-mile or three-mile walk or jog. Later, after work, I repeated the process. It turned out I was walking or jogging four or five miles a day. I also joined Jenny Craig and stayed on a fairly strict diet during that time. It turned out to be one of the better-unplanned things I did while I was there because during the eight months I lost 35 pounds, which was quite a surprise for my wife when I got to Melbourne.

When it came time for me to retire, after I had given them eight months to find a permanent replacement, I was surprised to find out one day that they wanted me to be that permanent replacement. The vice president of public affairs tried to convince me to continue in my present position with the likelihood that I would be promoted to staff vice president, but after a bit over 40 years, most of which were spent working in public affairs, and a lot of which were spent away from home, I finally made up my mind to retire.

Today General Dynamics Corporation looks much different than it did when I worked there. From 1952 until the early 1990s the company manufactured tanks, rockets, missiles, submarines, warships, fighter aircraft, and electronics for all of the American military services. In the early 1990s General Dynamics sold nearly all of its divisions except for Electric Boat and Land Systems. It got rid of almost all of its products except submarines and main battle tanks.

In the mid-1990s it began expanding again by acquiring combat vehicle-related businesses, information technology product and service companies, additional shipyards, and the Gulfstream Aerospace Corporation. Today General Dynamics is focused on its growth by continuing a relentless focus on operations and continuous improvement, expanding margins, increasing earnings and return on invested capital, and disciplined capital deployment.

The corporation once more has over 90,000 employees and had 2016 revenues of $31.4 billion. A GD fact sheet says all of its operation groups performed well in 2016, with solid demand for its products and services across its business . Its stock quote on January 16, 2018 was $210.26.

Retirement

Once I decided to really retire my wife was concerned about it. She was not sure we were ready for it financially or mentally. In my professional career I was noted as a bit of a workaholic. I put in long hours, studied hard, and endured the pressures that came with constantly working with the national and international news media.

Peggy was not sure I could handle the slow pace of retirement after all of the high-pressure jobs. But I was sure I could. I knew there were lots of things I could do to stay busy and mentally challenged and the thought of retirement did not phase me. In fact, it excited me.

I had known several Air Force pilots who had retired and gone from an extremely active and demanding life of daily challenges to a sedentary existence in which they did almost nothing. One even bought a houseboat and just sat on it for months at a time. The problem with going from a very active career to a period when you basically do nothing is that it isn't good for your health and you may not last long. Both of those colonels were dead in a year after they retired. They both died from natural causes, but I was always convinced they died because they no longer had the excitement and adrenaline rush they were used to in their Air Force careers.

I've known a lot of guys who were basically adrenaline addicts. They did things that scare other people, like driving high-speed cars or jumping out of airplanes or any number of things that give the body a severe jolt of adrenaline. Sometimes those guys don't last long when they retire unless they can find some way to keep up the adrenaline their body has been getting almost daily for many years.

I knew I wouldn't fall into that trap and planned to stay busy to keep my mind active and my fingers nimble on a computer keyboard. So, even before they had time to recruit a replacement for me I retired, jumped into my car and drove to Melbourne to begin a real retirement. And, in case you are wondering, I found other ways to keep busy and never missed the daily grind of constant telephone calls and questions from reporters.

CHAPTER 7
RETIREMENT IN FLORIDA

I wasn't sure retirement would be everything I wanted. I dreamed of a more relaxed lifestyle, with challenges I could decide for myself. I was absolutely confident we would be able to handle retirement financially. I had two retirements, one from the Air Force and one from General Dynamics Corporation, plus a small cash-out from AM General LLC, and in a bit more than five-years I would be eligible for full Social Security. I assured my wife we would have no financial worries in retirement. She was still worried about it, but I was not!

I was more concerned about the mental aspect of retirement. After watching others I had known die fairly quickly after they retired, I knew I had to keep busy. But first I wanted to take a brief vacation. I didn't want to go anywhere; I just wanted to take it easy.

In 1993 we had built a retirement home in Melbourne, FL and in November 1993 Peggy moved into our home while I was still working at General Dynamics Corporate headquarters. As I mentioned earlier, we built a four-bedroom, 2,400-square foot house with a pool and screened-in patio. One of the first things we did was to convert two of the bedrooms, one on each side of the house, into our own private office spaces. We bought an iMac computer for each of us and a printer we could share.

I wasn't ready to jump into any kind of work, although I had some ideas for freelancing some of my writing skills. Instead I wanted to take advantage of my free time to play some golf. Over the years I had enjoyed playing golf, especially at West Point and again in Thailand where my boss and I played occasionally. With my retirement I had an ideal opportunity to improve my game.

We live in an unincorporated area named Suntree, located a few miles north of the city limits of Melbourne. We had spent all of my vacation time for the last three years of my time at GDLS looking for a place to retire. We visited North and South Carolina, Georgia, and all of Florida, and we settled on Suntree, an unincorporated, planned community development located in a part of Brevard County, just off of Interstate 95, about midway between Miami and Jacksonville. There are only like homes in each sub-division, which meant that you will not find an $80,000 house sitting next to a $400,000 house.

In addition to being a beautifully planned community of about 10,000 people, it had Suntree Country Club, with two world-class golf courses, one of which was located across the street from our newly built house.

Golf at Suntree

The most wonderful attraction to Suntree Country Club was not its clubhouse, which was quite nice, but its two world-class golf courses. The Classic Course was a rather traditional 18-hole course that was always manicured to professional standards. In fact, the professional Seniors Tour included the Suntree Classic Course on its annual tour, and the first Ladies Professional Golf Association held its first tournament on the same course.

I was told by quite a few people who had many times watched the seniors play at Suntree, and had talked with several of the senior players, that professional golfers considered the Suntree Classic course to be one of the finest courses in Florida.

Soon after we arrived in Suntree and moved into our new house, which we built just for our retirement, we were able to watch the seniors play on the Classic Course. It was a joy to watch them play because they were so good. It was wonderful to see how our course was actually supposed to be played.

My favorite course, however, was the Challenge Course. It too was and still is a world-class course, but it had a lot more challenges than the Classic Course. The Challenge Course has water hazards on every hole, two on many holes, and three on a few holes. As you might guess it was and still is a real challenge and a thrill to play if you love golf.

One of the first things I did in retirement was join the golf club and buy a modified golf cart. The cart had a more powerful engine that made it possible to drive 35 mph on Suntree roads. I recognized that a traditional golf cart can only go about 15 mph and that is a road hazard. Even today sometimes there is a long line of cars waiting to pass a slowly moving golf cart on Suntree roads.

I joined a golf league that had members who were almost all at least as old as I was. We played in our league twice a week, but even that wasn't enough. For about two months I played every day and sometimes twice a day.

Our house is located on the back nine of the Challenge Course, so very often after we finished the 18-holes we would play the front nine again on the way home.

I say "we" because my wife played too. She joined a ladies league and played twice a week, but sometimes we would just go out together and play a round, especially on the weekends. She loved it as much as I did, and she was great off the tee, not so great with a putter. She would just about knock the cover off the ball from the tee, but sometimes three-and-four-putted on the greens.

When I started playing golf at Suntree I had a golf handicap of 24, which sometimes was embarrassing. But, over the course of several years I got it down to a 9; not as good as I would have liked but respectable. For 12 years I continued to play golf on the Suntree courses, as well as a few other local courses, until I had to give it up because of lower back problems that simply would not let me swing the clubs the way I wanted.

For those who may not know, the golf swing puts a lot of torque on your lower back and over time it weakens that part of the back and causes a lot of pain. If you watch professional golf on television, you may notice that most professional golfers eventually develop a lot of lower back problems.

I recently noticed that Tiger Woods has had several major back surgeries and has not played more than a few rounds in the last several years. It gets them all eventually. Not that I am comparing myself to a professional golfer. I played a lot but I remained a rank amateur.

One of the things that always bothered me and still does actually, is the proliferation of kids driving golf carts on our streets. Our county ordnance stipulates the following restrictions:

. The driver must be at last 14 years of age.
. Carrying more passengers than the cart was designed to carry is prohibited.
. The golf cart cannot be operated on bicycle paths or sidewalks.
. Golf carts may only cross roadways at designated pedestrian crossings.

There are other restrictions too, but these are the primary ones that are routinely violated. Too many parents allow children much younger than 14 to drive their golf carts on the street and kids often load the cart with other kids. I have frequently seen golf carts designed to carry two passenger carrying five kids. And one of the most intrusive violations is when kids and often adults drive their carts on the sidewalks because they fear driving in traffic with cars. Some even expect pedestrians to step off the sidewalk to get out of their way so the cart can pass.

I've seen police cars drive right past violators, when the violators should be stopped and warned. The reality is that a violation of any of the ordnances is punishable as a non-criminal traffic citation resulting in a fine. Fat chance! In 25 years I've never seen someone driving a cart stopped, a violator fined, or both. Nobody enforces the ordnances. I know it sounds petty, but traffic accidents with golf carts can be serious.

It is particularly aggravating to people who do not golf to be stuck behind a golf cart going 15 mph on streets having two yellow lines, which means the cars cannot legally pass the golf carts. I've seen as many as six cars in a line behind a golf cart, waiting to pass the thoughtless golfer who refused to move off the road at least long enough for the cars to pass.

While there are signs that say golf carts and cars must share the roadway, golf carts are designed to be driven off-road on courses. It is a matter of courtesy for a golfer to move off of the road to allow the cars to pass, but many simply refuse to do so!

Freelancing my consulting efforts

After a few months of golf I decided it was time for me to find something more constructive to occupy my time, so I contacted General Dynamics Corporation to see if there was any contract consulting work I might be able to do for them. It turned out the public affairs department was thinking about the same thing at the same time. The vice-president of public affairs was interested in having someone put together a history of General Dynamics Corporation, including all of its integral parts, so he hired me to research and write a comprehensive history of the corporation.

It was a difficult chore because throughout its history General Dynamics Corporation had so many parts. While their antecedents go back to the 19th century, the current corporation began in 1952. Nevertheless, I researched the entire history from 1859 to1997 before I began writing and included a historical lineage section to the history I wrote.

The research was tedious because there were so many parts and each part branched off into new parts until the corporation was established in 1952. I coordinated with the public affairs/communications personnel at each major division and they gathered significant dates from their division executives that they thought should be included in a history of their division.

Even limiting the current history to the beginning in 1952, it was difficult to piece together all of the parts leading to what existed in 1997, the year I wrote the history. And each separate part had significant dates that needed to be included in the history.

As is usually the case on such projects, it is impossible to satisfy everyone. Some executives loved the history I put together and some did not. Those who did not were primarily upset because I didn't include enough of the dates they considered significant. Without acknowledging it, some executives thought I should have included much more focus on their division.

Additional Freelance Work

I had spent weeks working on the special project at the corporate headquarters in Falls Church, Virginia and was glad to get back home. For a while I returned to the golf course, playing every day. I also wrote a lot of letters-to-the-editor at *Florida Today*, a local Gannett daily morning newspaper. I also wrote a lot of op-ed articles for *Florida Today*, as well as *TC Palm*, which was a Scripps daily newspaper, that has since become a member of the Gannett family, and *Vero's Voice Magazine* a high quality monthly community magazine published in Vero Beach, Florida.

For a long time *Florida Today* published many of my op-ed articles. In fact, for a few years it published 25 or 30 a year. It didn't pay anything but I didn't care. It was a way for me to reach our local community about issues I cared about. Recently they changed management and publication of my articles slowed down considerably. I don't really know why, other than the fact that the newspaper has gotten a lot smaller and has noticeably reduced publishing op-ed articles.

A few months after I returned to Florida from working with General Dynamics as a free-lance contract writer, I contacted a former Air Force friend who retired and had been handling public relations for Pratt & Whitney in

Florida. I asked him if he might need to hire out some of his writing chores, and it turned out he did. He hired me to write a series of articles on Pratt & Whitney aircraft engines that could be translated into Arabic to be published in the United Arab Emirates (UAE) Air Force Magazine.

Over a period of several months I wrote articles on their aircraft engines, as well as on Pratt & Whitney and its parent, United Technologies Corporation. The articles were compiled into a special report on Pratt & Whitney filling an entire issue of the *UAE Air Force Magazine*. United Technologies was previously headquartered in Hartford, Connecticut but toward the end of 2015 moved its headquarters to Farmington, Connecticut. During my research on Pratt & Whitney aircraft engines, I visited UTC's corporate headquarters in Hartford to do research on the corporation and the Pratt & Whitney headquarters in East Hartford, Connecticut, to research the company that paid me to write the articles.

Unfortunately, shortly after I completed the series of articles on the aircraft engines my contact at Pratt & Whitney retired and the work project stopped.

What I discovered shortly after I retired was that absence does not make the heart grow fonder, or out of sight out of mind, or any one of a number of other clichés. The point is the further you get from retirement the less frequently your old contacts think of you, which is another way to say my freelance work dried up over a period of a few years.

I didn't miss getting work from a financial standpoint. As I had predicted to my wife our finances were sound. I didn't need the money as much as I needed the work to help me fill my days.

There was a serendipitous piece of good luck with the Pratt & Whitney work. I was introduced to the *UAE Air Force Magazine* editor. He liked the articles I had submitted for his magazine on the Pratt & Whitney engines and asked me if I might like to write some freelance articles on other defense industry products.

Of course, I jumped at that opportunity and wrote many articles for him treating such defense equipment as the HMMWV, the Abrams MBT, the 5-ton trucks, the Fox NBC reconnaissance vehicle, and an assortment of other defense-related products. Most of my articles would then be translated into Arabic and included in their magazine. This led to exposure throughout the Middle East, and the next thing I knew other doors opened for writing defense related articles for other Arab commercial newspapers. Of course I made sure there was nothing sensitive or classified in any of my articles.

After about a year of writing for Arab publications I decided to quit that venue because it sometimes took months to get paid. The editors would drag out payment as though they thought I might forget about it eventually. Instead I notified my Arab contacts that they would have to find someone else to write their articles. I got tired of sending inquiries to them about payment.

Since retirement I had made some new friends in Florida. One of them is Marshall Frank, a genuine renaissance man. He is a 30-year retired Miami-Dade homicide detective, who spent a lot of years working Crime Scene Investigations (CSI). I love to listen to him talk about his work, which was more interesting than anything we see on television programs such as "CSI" or "NCIS." Not that he tells me anything sensitive or classified, just interesting stuff.

Marshall is also a concert violinist who played 1st chair in a symphony orchestra for a while. He is absolutely wonderful on the violin even after all these years, and he is nearly my age. Just as impressive, he is a published author and has written 14 books, is a marvelous conversationalist with an engaging personality and is principally responsible for a local organization that supports and promotes the development of young preteen and teenagers who have exceptional musical talents. He is quite simply a true renaissance man, who I am proud to call my friend!

He writes op-ed articles for the same publications I do. One day about five years ago he called me and commented that since we both write for the same publications, we ought to get together for breakfast some time. So we met for breakfast and enjoyed each other's company. A close friendship developed and we've been going to breakfast about once a week ever since. Along the way another friend started joining us, so now three of us get together. Sometimes a fourth friend joins us and we figuratively solve all the world problems over bacon, eggs, oatmeal, toast, and coffee.

Marshall Frank is the primary reason I've written books. One day while we were eating breakfast he said, "You've written a lot of articles for newspapers and magazines, you ought to try your hand at writing a book." Well, many years ago I tried to write a novel and discovered I had no talent for it. I simply did not have an ear for realistic dialogue. But I had never tried to write a book of non-fiction.

Writing Books

I decided to take my friend's advice and thought about writing a book of non-fiction, but first I took a seminar he teaches on how to write and get published. I wasn't sure what to write about, but when I thought about it seriously, it occurred to me that I had witnessed a lot of changes in our society over the previous 70 years, and there was an audience of potential readers who hadn't lived through that same period. With that in mind, I did a lot of research and wrote my first book about major changes to our society during about a 60-year period. Some people don't realize that it takes a lot longer to do the research than it does to write the book.

I titled my first book *America: A Cultural Enigma*. The title sets people back initially until I remind them that an enigma is a mystery, and it is a bit of a mystery why and how we have changed so dramatically as a society during such a relatively short period.

Think about it! We went from a time when the sequence was courtship, marriage, and family to a period when the sequence has changed to courtship, sexual experimentation, cohabitation, pregnancy, separation and maybe new courtship, but rarely marriage.

We went from a period when divorce was extremely unusual and carried a stigma, to a period when nearly 50% of marriages end in divorce; from a period when out-of-wedlock births were rare and carried a huge stigma to a period in 2012 in which *National Review* says that 40.7 percent of all births were out-of-wedlock. "Among non-Hispanic blacks, the figure is highest, at 72.2 percent; for American Indians/Alaska Natives, it's 66.9 percent; 53.5 percent for Hispanics; 29.4 percent for non-Hispanic whites; and a mere 17.1 percent for Asians/Pacific Islanders."

My first book also treated such items as racism, medical advances, life expectancy, growth of the Islamic influence and threat, national defense, abortion, homosexuality, capital punishment, violence in America, our addiction to technology, foreign cars, and a host of other hot topics.

Once I finished the draft of my new book, I set about trying to find a publisher. Much to my friend's shock and mine too I found a publisher quickly. When you think about it that is really unusual.

Many people who write books send their manuscripts to sometimes hundreds of potential publishers and more often than not are unlikely to ever get published unless they self-publish. I sent mine to fewer than a dozen publishers and very quickly got a response from Black Rose Writing. It was a fairly new independent publishing house located in Texas whose owner/editor strongly believes in developing a personal relationship with his authors.

I first sent a letter of inquiry with a synopsis of what I proposed as a book of non-fiction. Black Rose Writing responded saying it was interested and wanted to see an outline and sample chapter, which I provided. I was next advised to send the manuscript, which I did. Shortly after that I received in the mail a contract for it to publish my book.

This surprised my friend who had published 14 books, but had never known anyone to get a positive response so quickly.

What stunned me was how wonderful it was to work with the editor/owner. He was helpful, quick to respond, and produced a beautiful cover for my new book. I have since written, and he has published, three more of my books, all of which are about America. I absolutely love our country and enjoy writing about it. Interestingly enough each book led to another. Thoughts planted in one book led to the concept for the next.

One reviewer on Amazon.com said "I found this to be an excellent book and recommend it to everyone! " Another Amazon reviewer said, "...In closing, this is a book that everyone, from the young adult to the seasoned veteran can enjoy time and time again."

My second book, *America: Where Great Things Happen,* is about wonderfully exciting things Americans do that we rarely hear about because the news media focuses almost exclusively on negative stories. Every single day wonderful things happen in our country, but one would never know it by watching the news. The philosophy that seems to drive headlines is, "If it bleeds, it leads."

We are blasted out of our chairs daily by television commentators announcing "breaking news," which is almost always negative. Pay close attention to the evening television news. My guess is you will find about 30 seconds of positive news and the rest is negative. You won't find that in *America: Where Great Things Happen.* Instead, you will find uplifting and inspirational tales that bring a smile to your face and make you proud to be an American.

One reader described it by saying "I thoroughly enjoyed reading this book. It left me with a good feeling and I would absolutely recommend it to anyone who enjoys current events and really just anyone who needs a pick me up. There really is good in the world." Another noted, "sit back, read and enjoy. It will lift your spirits and touch your heart."

My third book, *America: An Exceptional Nation,* explains why I believe American Exceptionalism is a truly defensible term that describes a nation blessed by our Creator with attributes that set the United States apart from much of the world.

It sometimes deals with the concept of political correctness, but it is not a political treatise. It is simply an explanation of why I believe in American Exceptionalism, and why I think that in their hearts most Americans share that belief. It explains why I am convinced America represents one of a handful of nations that can offer real hope for our world in the 21st Century. It offers a perspective that will make the reader feel good about America.

One reader offered "it is always so refreshing to read a book that has positive things to say about America instead of what we hear in the media so often today that tells of how awful this country is." Another wrote that Gilleland's third book is an unabashed profession of his love of the United States and why it became and still is the leader of the free world."

o   o   o

My fourth book, *America: A Conflicted Nation* is a discussion of issues about which Americans feel conflicted. Being conflicted is about feeling positive and negative about something at the same time, and being unable to shake off the uncomfortable feeling it produces.

For instance, as a country we are enormously proud of our immigrant history, yet we are frightened of what immigrants from the Middle East might bring with them to America. We are also conflicted about our military. Nearly everyone believes we need and should have a world class military, but what we are conflicted about is how much of our national treasure should be devoted to it. America is a truly extraordinary country, but there are many things that leave us feeling uneasy.

Trying to read the tealeaves is frustrating because many economists don't agree on our future. Those divergent views leave many of us wondering if anyone really knows what our future holds. However convoluted our future appears, we

179

must always remember that most of the world looks to us for moral guidance and a strong sense of what is right and wrong.

Much of the world focuses on us for leadership. They expect us to set the example and to lend a hand whenever it is needed. Many Americans feel conflicted about our country's role in the world, as well as how we address national issues that affect only our own residents.

One reader described this book as thought provoking, "a book everyone should read." Another described it as "a great book for the times."

Each of my publishing experiences with Black Rose Writing has been easier, more exciting, and more satisfying than I ever expected it to be. My publisher recently put all four books together into a Kindle Edition series titled *The America Series*, which sells for $5.99.

My writing experience has been like starting a new career. While it is not very profitable because I am not a well-known author, it has been a grand experience that I would recommend to anyone who thinks he or she has the raw talent to produce something that might have a chance of being published. I would also recommend Black Rose Writing to anyone who is uncertain where to send his or her manuscript.

Incidentally, all of my books are reviewed on Amazon.com, and virtually all of them received five-star ratings. I encourage you to go to Amazon.com, type in my name and see what readers' thought of my books.

My fifth book, which I'm writing now, *Stars, Stripes, and Corporate Logos*, is a memoir of much of my life, personal as well as professional. I've divided the chapters into sections that mostly stand-alone so the reader can jump around. I know I love to read, and I keep three or four books going all the time and sometimes I jump around from one book to another. And when I read good books I'm reminded how fertile the human mind is and how rewarding it can be to visualize what authors intend for their readers.

I have friends and family members who are not as devoted to reading as I am, which is difficult for me to understand. I cannot envision a world without books.

Chapter 8
Writing Satisfies the Soul

Now that I've told you I write Op-Ed and feature articles and books, it might be appropriate to explain how and why I became interested in writing and how I got started. I never deliberately decided to be a writer. I actually stumbled on to it accidentally as a way to let the world know how I felt about some issues I thought were important.

In 1983 and 1984 I tired of reading so many articles and letters-to-the-editor in California newspapers and magazines that were so critical of the military. After spending so much of my adult life serving in the military and watching citizens in other countries who would love to have the kind of world-class military we have, it was difficult for me to understand how so many of our citizens just didn't "get it."

A president's first responsibility is to keep his country free and secure. If he fails at that responsibility none of the social programs that our citizens love so much will matter. One need only study life in many other countries to verify that. So many people in other countries struggle under despotic governments where citizens have few options about how they will live. There are few countries in the world that offer citizens so many options to choose from, as we in the United States are blessed with.

When I think about all the ways I am blessed, being born a citizen of the United States ranks at the very top of that list. Nothing else even comes close to it.

To keep our country free and secure we must outfit a strong military, and that costs a lot of money. Our 44th president spent eight years virtually dismantling our military, reducing the defense budget to about six percent of the federal budget, which is the smallest amount in real terms during the previous 20 years. In dollar amounts it is higher than some years because of inflation, but as a percentage of the national budget it is lower than it was in 1996

It appeared to me that many of the letter writers thought the defense budget was too much, no matter what the dollar amount actually was. For those who just don't understand, any amount of money spent on national defense is wasted. For them it appears that our entire federal budget should be dedicated to social programs. It seemed uncanny to me that so many people didn't seem to understand that it is almost impossible to keep a free and secure nation without a strong, world-class military. And without a free and secure nation there won't be any social programs. Many of the letters-to-the-editor include so much misinformed and prejudiced information that I think somebody ought to correct the deluge of bad data being fed to the American public. So, in my small way I do what I can.

According to NationalPriorities.org, by far the lion's share of the federal budget goes to pay for mandatory spending, 64.63%, while discretionary spending, of which the defense budget is a part, accounts for only 29.35%.

I often discuss the letters and articles with friends who often complain about the fact that nobody seems to care about how uninformed citizens and celebrities are bombarding the print and broadcast media with tripe. But, few people I know seem to be interested in presenting an "alternative set of facts" to reach out to people who get much if not most of their information from the general media.

That's how it began. After a while, I got fed up with all the garbage I was reading in the newspapers and started writing. Initially, in a kind of exploratory way, I started writing letters-to-the-editor at various newspapers up and down the coast of California responding directly to specific authors, some well known and some unknown.

As explained earlier, I began by writing letters about the nuclear freeze issue. Later I branched out and wrote letters about our national defense posture generally. I was never contacted by any of the editors but they seemed to be very receptive because they ran almost everything I sent to them. I wrote about many issues, not just defense-related topics. The more I got published the more I wanted to use the newspapers to reach out to their readers.

I moved on from the nuclear freeze issue, to a criticism I levied against folks who always seem to think property owners should pay for everything through real estate taxes. I raised the question of double jeopardy as it related to the incongruity of one jury finding O.J. Simpson financially liable for a crime that another jury found him not guilty of committing. I wrote about the insanity of crediting Christopher Columbus with the discovery of America, which was already inhabited by millions of native citizens, especially since there is adequate evidence that suggest Leif Erickson, a Viking explorer, visited North America hundreds of years before Columbus.

I asked how you could credit someone with discovering what was already an inhabited continent, especially since Columbus never even visited the United States. He got lost on his way to India and landed on an island that is now part of the Bahamas, 10,000 miles short of his goal.

I wrote about the paucity of American flags flying on homes on national holidays. I generally set pen to paper whenever something bothered me, and instead of whining about the topic to friends and neighbors, I called attention to the issue to a much wider audience. Often I would get reader responses to my letters, and sometimes I would get telephone calls from readers who found my name in the local telephone directory.

After a while I began to think if I expanded my writing to include Op-Ed articles or lengthier feature articles, I might be able to reach more people with broader concepts and more facts. And it worked! I began to explore my writing options and found there were quite a few specialty magazines that welcomed unsolicited manuscripts. Next thing I knew I was being published in periodicals well beyond the Los Angeles area. I wrote articles for *The Sacramento Union* and *San Diego Union* on the myth of excessive defense spending. I was getting published fairly often up and down the coast of California.

I continued my writing long after I retired from the Air Force and expanded the topics I felt comfortable exploring. I discovered there were almost a limitless number of issues to be discussed if I spent the necessary time researching topics of interest. I found that few people I knew had any idea how much more time it takes to research an article than it takes to write it.

I co-wrote a lengthy article with a friend for *National Aeronautics* magazine on military aircraft. By lengthy I mean nearly 5,000 words, rather the traditional 500-600 words for newspaper Op-Ed articles. That article was well received by defense officials in the Washington, DC area.

I continued to write articles for defense-oriented specialty magazines, especially describing the performance characteristics and capabilities of military equipment. I wrote articles on the HMMWV, Abrams MBT, the Fox Nuclear Biological and Chemical (NBC) Reconnaissance Vehicle, the wisdom of dropping atomic bombs on Hiroshima and Nagasaki to end World War II, and a wide assortment of other defense-related articles.

They appeared in magazines such as the *Journal of Defense & Diplomacy, Armoured Vehicles* (a British magazine), *Military Technology, Third World Defence* (a British magazine), *Emirate News* (an English language Arab newspaper), and many other periodicals, both domestic and international. It seemed like the more I wrote the wider the distribution and a more extensive audience I reached.

Over the years my defense-oriented articles appeared in major international newspapers and magazines in Egypt, England, France, Japan, Sweden, Thailand, and the United Arab Emirates. In the United States they appeared in major newspapers and magazines in California, Illinois, Michigan, Indiana, New York, Virginia, and Washington, DC.

In the United States I wrote general interest articles on additional topics such as the Persian Gulf oil, our misplaced guilt over Hiroshima, our "fuelish" habits (oil), the need to carry out executions more humanely or not at all, the need for more sanity in our foreign affairs policy, our dependence on gasoline, scientific explanation for intelligent design, UFOs, movie reviews, illegal immigrants, the cancelled F-22 program, the need for a rational discussion on our health care, high technology in our homes, whether burning our flag is protected speech, singing the motor city blues, and the need for a missile defense shield. The latter topic received a lot of attention.

It might be worthwhile to relate a few things about that here. We live in a world that only science fiction writers dreamed about until recently. The potential destruction that evil forces can unleash on us is almost unlimited. And we are powerless to defend against some of it.

Twenty-one countries are suspected of having ballistic missiles, including China, India, Iran, Iraq, North Korea, Pakistan, and Russia. In the wrong hands, these missiles could unleash unbelievable horror on the United States.

Unfortunately, we are somewhat impotent against such an attack, and the potential consequences are almost too horrific to imagine. This is not a hypothetical hazard; it's a very real possibility. The Department of Defense has been working to develop a missile defense system for more than 30 years, but because of budgetary and political constraints, progress has been slow.

Ballistic missiles are potentially the terrorist's ultimate weapon. All the posturing over the possibility of Iran developing a single nuclear weapon or North Korea testing an intercontinental ballistic missile that can reach the United States may seem like a lot of fuss. However, an electromagnetic pulse (EMP) attack on America's electronic infrastructure could bring the country to its knees, and it is possible for only one inter-continental ballistic missile to do that.

EMP attacks are generated when a nuclear weapon is detonated at altitudes a few dozen kilometers above the Earth's surface. The explosion of even a small nuclear warhead could produce a set of electromagnetic pulses to interact with the earth's atmosphere and the earth's magnetic field.

According to Lowell Wood, acting chairman of the Commission to Assess the Threat to the United States from an EMP Attack, "these electromagnetic pulses propagate from the burst point of the nuclear weapon to the line of sight on the earth's horizon, potentially covering a vast geographic region at the speed of light." For example, a nuclear weapon detonated at an altitude of 400 kilometers above the central United States could blanket our entire country, as well as parts of Canada and Mexico.

Over the years, Newt Gringrich has frequently warned Americans about the threat to our country from nuclear weapons. On March 29, 2009, Gringrich said,

"One to three missiles tipped with nuclear weapons and armed to detonate at a high altitude...would create an EMP 'overlay' that triggers a continent-wide collapse of our entire electrical, transportation, and communications infrastructure.

"Those who claim that there is little to fear from Iran or North Korea, because 'at best' they will have only one or two nuclear weapons, ignore the catastrophic level of threat we now face from just a couple of nuclear weapons."

Can you even imagine what life would be like today without electricity? Just let your mind wander a bit with that concept. Think about all things in your home that require electricity; now extrapolate that to cover our entire country. Perhaps you can see why I think it is so important to continue writing about some of these national security issues.

When I retired and moved to Florida I continued to write, and during the next 25 years I had over 300 articles published in *Florida Today* and 60 articles in *TC Palm,* with a sampling included in *Vero Voice Magazine,* published in Vero Beach, Florida. Of course a lot of my articles continued to be published in other United States and international publications too.

So far more than 500 of them have been published and that number grows every year. I don't say that to brag, but to illustrate my efforts to reach the

American public with topically sensitive subjects that I think need serious discussion.

Radical Islam, Abortion, & Campaign Finance Reform

Two of my favorite topics to write about are radical Islam and abortion. It is very difficult to get our news media to print any articles that are even remotely negative about Islam. Like most Americans, the news media tends to treat Islam as just another religion and they don't want to print anything that smacks of religious intolerance. They don't seem to appreciate that Islam is an ideology, a consuming way of life that includes religion, but is much, much more.

I feel no animus toward Muslims either racially or ethnically. In fact, a Muslim doctor saved my life in 2007 while I was touring Jordan. I became deathly ill in Amman from severe dehydration due to food poisoning. The doctor drove to a restaurant to pick up my wife and me, took us across town to his clinic, and treated me with antibiotics and IVs for about five hours, after which he drove us across town to our hotel. At about 10:00 p.m. he returned to our hotel and treated me again with an IV and an additional antibiotic shot. The next morning he contacted us in Israel to follow-up on my condition. I have the utmost respect and admiration for that doctor. His treatment of me was particularly impressive because the day he treated me was the last day of Ramadan and he was expected to spend the day with his family. Instead he devoted much of the day to treating me, an individual his belief system called an infidel!

My problem is with the Quran, which is the Muslim holy book that directs much of what you see radical Muslims doing in the world. Sura 9.5 gives Muslims only three options for dealing with infidels (non-Muslims): convert them, enslave them and collect tribute (*Jizya tax*), or kill them. There are no other options. The Quran also forbids a Muslim from having a non-Muslim as a friend, although it encourages Muslims to lie to further Islam, so a Muslim can pretend to be your friend.

Sura 5:33 says "The punishment of those who wage war against Allah and His messenger and strive to make mischief in the land is only this, that they should be murdered or crucified or their hands and their feet should be cut off on opposite sides or they should be imprisoned; this shall be as a disgrace for them in this world, and in the hereafter they shall have a grievous chastisement."

Sura 8:12 says, "I will cast terror into the hearts of those who disbelieve. Therefore strike off their heads and strike off every fingertip of them"

Sura 9:14 says, "Fight against them so that Allah will punish them by your hands and disgrace them and give you victory over them and heal the breasts of a believing people."

Humiliating and hurting non believers not only has the blessing of Allah, but it is ordered as a means of carrying out his punishment and even "healing" the hearts of Muslims.

Sura 18:65-81 rationalizes honor killings in which a family member is murdered because he or she (most typically she) brought shame to the family either through apostasy or perceived moral indiscretion.

Nowhere in the Quran does it say to love your neighbor. However, there are over 100 verses that call Muslims to war with nonbelievers for the sake of Islamic rule. Some are quite graphic, with commands to chop off heads and fingers and kill infidels wherever they may be hiding.

The Muslim Brotherhood, which is in the international news a lot lately, is a transnational Islamic organization established in 1928. It has a 100-year-plan to establish a worldwide caliphate in which Sharia law will apply to everyone. If that happens, our Constitutional guarantees and Christian and Jewish beliefs will be meaningless because they are incompatible with Sharia law.

Since 1968 there have been so many major events in which radical Muslims have attacked innocent civilians around the world that airport security conducts random searches of 80-year-old women, little kids, and airline pilots with proper identification, Secret Service agents who are members of the president's security detail, 85-year old people with metal hips, and Medal of Honor winners, but they cannot pay special attention to Muslims lest they be guilty of profiling.

Anyone who takes issue with any aspect of the Quran or Hadith (a report that describes the words, actions, or habits of the Islamic prophet Muhammad) is called an Islamaphobe, whether or not they feel any animus against Muslims. One need only read the Islamic holy book, the Quran, to see that most of the things the so-called radicals do is directed by their holy book. The so-called peaceful Muslims simply do not strictly follow the dictates of the Quran.

Peaceful Muslims who do not precisely follow all of the dictates of the Quran are somewhat like Roman Catholics who practice contraception, or have abortions, or both, even though Catholic dogma strictly forbids those actions. The Catholic Church teaches that those practices are mortal sins. Nevertheless many, if not most, Catholics who practice contraception and/or have abortions consider themselves to be faithful Catholics. Thus it is with Muslims who do not precisely follow all of the dictates of the Quran.

My relationship with God became increasingly important to me after the Islamic attack on September 11, 2001, when 19 radical Muslim terrorists flew commercial aircraft into the World Trade Center and the Pentagon, and crashed one aircraft in a Pennsylvania field. It brought home the reality that on any given day disaster could strike our country, and life is tenuous at best.

Everyone was shocked by that disaster. But, once the shock wore off, we had to adjust to frightening concepts that took many of us by surprise.

All 19 of the al-Qaeda terrorists were radical Muslims, intent on killing Americans. They succeeded beyond their wildest dreams, and much of the Muslim world celebrated. Television coverage depicted men and women rejoicing in the streets around the world because the terrorists had wrought such massive destruction on a country many thought was indestructible.

Until then, many Americans gave very little thought to the concept of Islam. Most probably thought it was just another religion, with a large U.S. population living in Dearborn, MI.

Muslims believe Islam is the supreme religion, and all other religions are false religions that represent infidels. The problem is that most Americans don't know very much about Islam. Comparatively few have ever seen a Qu'ran, let alone read one. They don't know or don't realize that Sura 9.5 (Suras are like chapters in a Bible) in the Qu'ran applies to all Muslims, not just radical Muslims.

The Muslim Brotherhood, which has been in the news a lot lately, is a transnational movement founded in 1928. It has a 100-year plan to transform the world into a caliphate, in which Sharia Law would govern everyone. Under that scenario our Constitutional rights and Judeo/Christian beliefs would be meaningless, because Sharia law is not compatible with them.

Hamas and Hezbollah are the most widely known outgrowths of the Muslim Brotherhood, all three of which call for the complete destruction of Israel and the U.S.

These facts have surely been known to our intelligence networks for a long time; however, what the American public has learned in the last ten years is that millions of good Muslims, who don't strictly follow the tenants of the Qu'ran live among us. These Muslims mean us no harm, wishing only to live harmoniously in a country that offers wonderful opportunities for families, neighbors and friends.

However, the Muslim population in the U.S. is estimated to be between three to eight million. If only one-half of one percent of them want to harm us, that is between 15,000 and 40,000 potential domestic terrorists. Not an insignificant number! And Islam is growing in the United States.

According to CNS News, there has been a 74 percent increase ion U.S. Mosques in the past 15 years. The number of mosques has grown from 1,209 in 2001 to well over 3,000 in 2018.

I write about radical Islam frequently because I consider it to be one of the most dangerous threats to our future and it appears most Americans do not recognize the threat.

Nevertheless, the major lesson since the 9/11/2001 attack on our World Trade Center and the Pentagon is that we must all embrace each other and find a way to share this bountiful and wonderful country, or we will surely perish together.

Abortion

As for abortion, it is perhaps the most difficult topic of all to write about because our country is so divided on this issue that no matter what is written about it, a sizable portion of the public will disagree. It is an explosive issue that receives an enormous amount of attention in the news media. It raises its controversial head center stage in almost all political discussions about health care programs. Progressives want contraceptive options and abortions covered in the government's health care plan, while conservatives want no federal money spent on abortions anywhere.

There is no consensus, but there are reasonable arguments on both sides of this contentious issue, although one could argue that the deliberate taking of an innocent human life is always immoral. A recent Gallup poll found that 53 percent of those surveyed approved of abortion under certain conditions. Only 23 percent approved of it under all circumstances. Twenty-two percent believe abortion should be illegal in all circumstances. Many people view abortion in absolute terms. They believe it is either infanticide (murder) or a woman's right to decide about her own body. In truth it may be somewhere in between, because there is more at stake than a woman's body.

Abortion is an intensely personal issue about which each side claims to be on the side of the angels. Notice that everyone is for something and no one is against anything; thus, we have such catch phrases as pro-life and pro-choice. *Inclusio unius est exclusion alterius* (the inclusion is the exclusion of the other).

Some people believe women should have complete control of their own bodies, concluding that unborn babies are nothing more than an insensate non-viable collection of human tissue that needs no representation in these discussions.

Of course a sonogram early in pregnancy will dispel this myth, as does microsurgery performed on babies still in the womb. A fetus is a distinctly separate individual with its own blood type and DNA, and the question that must be addressed is, who speaks for the baby.

Those who doubt the fetus is a baby should watch a video available on the Internet at www.ted.com, titled *From Conception to Birth*. It is a time lapsed video taken in the womb during a pregnancy. It lasts only 60 seconds, but it is an eye opener. It includes time lapsed images from fertilization of an egg through the birth of a baby—live coverage. The images of the baby during the entire birthing process are extremely powerful and disprove the myth that a fetus is not a baby.

I personally believe our national focus has been wrong for many years. Instead of focusing on a woman's right to have an abortion, we should have been focusing on contraception. By far the majority of abortions are simply a matter to which some women resort when they and their partner, for whatever reason, do not want to accept responsibility for the consequences of their moment of passion. Pregnancy is always a possibility when two members of the opposite sex have unprotected sexual intercourse. But in the throes of passion millions of people forget about protection or just decide to "chance it."

With all the contraceptive options available today, with the exception of rape, no woman should ever get pregnant unless she wants to have a baby. After all, it is far better to prevent pregnancy than it is to abort a baby, and it only takes a modest effort to exercise contraceptive prudence, especially since the advent of the "morning after" pill, which incidentally might prevent pregnancy even in the event of rape.

Campaign Finance Reform

Another thorny topic I have frequently written about is the subject of campaign finance reform. The cost of politics has become obscene. Consider that the annual salary for Florida's governor is $130,000, yet Governor Scott spent over $85 million to get that job. The annual salary for the president of the United States is $400,000; yet presidential candidates and their national party routinely spend over $1 billion dollars to get that job.

Don't look for anything to change any time soon. During the 2016 presidential election campaigns, the two primary candidates, both champions of the lower and middle-class, spent a combined amount of $3 billion to get a job that pays an annual salary of $400,000. Does that make any sense? Well it does if you consider it is power that motivates the candidates, not money. For them the sound of success is not a ringing cash register, but a gavel that tells them the election is over and one of them won!

What surprises me even more is that the American public doesn't seem to care. After many years of promising campaign finance reform politicians continue to spend outrageous amounts of money to get elected, and I don't expect that to change any time soon. I continue to write about this phenomenon but to little effect. Once elections are over the public seems to go back to sleep on the subject of campaign finance reform.

National Debt

Another timely topic I like to write about is our national debt, which is approaching $20 trillion. Can the federal budget be balanced and national debt reduced without taking draconian steps? Yes! Draconian steps are not necessary, if by draconian we mean unusually severe, harsh, or cruel. We have to face the realities of our nation's financial crisis and make hard choices, but that simply means our government has to do the same things we expect of our citizens.

What do we tell anyone who digs a financial hole they can't seem to get out of? Live within your means! Quit spending more money than you earn. Cut up your credit cards and slowly pay off their balances.

Nobody wants higher taxes or cuts to our entitlement programs, but our national addiction to spending is insane and has to stop. To start, we need a Constitutional amendment requiring a balanced budget. But a balanced budget won't pay down the national debt. We need to structure a budget surplus. So, our second priority must be to spend less than we earn. That will require cuts to government programs, reasonable cuts, not draconian cuts.

The Right Post lists 10 common sense steps to balancing the budget without raising taxes. I've altered them somewhat. Nobody will like them, but they are not draconian.

1) Limit Social Security cost of living increases
2) Gradually increase the Social Security entitlement age to 70
3) Modestly increase the Medicare deductible
4) Reduce or eliminate farm subsidies
5) Close some of our overseas military bases
6) Cut the number of government employees
7) Eliminate earmarks
8) Eliminate welfare for illegal immigrants
9) Limit discretionary spending to the rate of inflation
10) Curb Medicare waste.

Obviously, there are other areas where prudent cuts could also be made. But in the aggregate, these I've mentioned would reduce federal spending by more than $300 billion per year, without dramatically changing our standard of living.

Any cuts will be painful for some people, but draconian cuts and tax increases are not necessary. In my writing experience, you get grief whenever you suggest cuts to pet projects. The truth is everyone would like us to balance the budget and reduce the debt, but only if it doesn't cost them anything. Everyone seems to think it can all be done if we just take more money from the wealthy. The truth is that we could confiscate every penny wealthy people have and it still wouldn't begin to meet our financial needs. I suspect it is a problem we will live with forever.

Other Items of Interest

I also continue to submit articles to international publications. Even today I continue to write on topics that interest me and expect to do so for as long as I can sit in front of a computer and bang out stories on my keyboard—as long as editors of national and international publications are willing to publish them.

As mentioned earlier more than 500 of my articles, as well as more than 1,000 letters-to-the-editor, have been published in newspapers all over the United States.

What always interests me are telephone calls I receive every time one of my articles appears in a local newspaper. I am the only Gilleland in our local telephone directory so no one has any trouble finding me. I haven't kept tabs on the callers, but I'm going to guess about 90 percent of the calls are congratulatory, while only about 10 percent are negative. The positive ones tend to be very complimentary, while the negative ones can be really nasty.

I always explain to the callers that I appreciate their feedback, and it doesn't bother me when people disagree with something I write. The whole point of writing articles is to stimulate public discussion of topically sensitive issues. It doesn't matter if the caller agrees with me. What matters is that I got his or her attention about something we both care about and hopefully the caller will continue discussing the topics with his or her friends and acquaintances.

I even encourage those who call to write something for the newspapers or magazines, either critical or complimentary, that addresses the same topic. I'm serious when I explain to readers that writing is truly good for the soul.

I feel good just knowing I have touched people and made them think about something I believe is important. I have come to believe it does no good to just sit home and complain to your spouse about something you feel strongly about. Hit the typewriter or computer and share your thoughts with a much wider audience or call a radio or television commentator and let him or her know what you think about a topic.

Democracy vs. Representative Republic

Lately I feel compelled to pick up my pen or sit down at my computer every time I hear some politician refer to our nation as a Democracy. It is not now nor has it ever been a democracy. They always like to call us a democracy because that registers well with their constituents.

Far too many people do not know the difference between a democracy and a representative republic. We no longer teach government in high school civics classes and the consequence is that too many people, including our elected officials, do not realize that we are not now and have never been a democracy. They like to cite democracy because the concept of majority rule is so popular and is generally preferred by those who get really upset when they or their cause loses elections to Electoral College votes. Hillary Clinton and her supporters were a prime example of that in the 2016 presidential election.

A pure democracy is basically majority rule. If we lived in a democracy three or four of our most populated states (New York, California., Texas, Florida) would control everything and the rest of us could just stay home from the polls. Our Founding Fathers knew that, so they set up a representative republic in which each state gets representation (two senators and a representative number of congressional representatives) so that every state participates in our government equally. They established the Electoral College to decide our national election for the same reason.

Since Hillary Clinton won California by some three million votes and won the national election by about three million popular votes, in a pure democracy she would now be the president. But, because each state has a representative number of electoral votes Donald Trump won by a huge margin of electoral votes. Thus 51 jurisdictions, including Washington, DC, elected the president, instead of just California. It has been this way since our founding as a nation.

Perhaps it's time to reinstate civics classes in our high schools and colleges, although I suspect some of the protestors know the difference between a democracy and a representative republic, but just don't care. Their disappointment over not getting their way is more important to them than a basic understanding of the process for electing national leaders.

On Becoming an Uncivil Nation

Over the years I have also been invited to radio talk shows and occasionally to local television program. That just isn't something I focus on, but when a broadcast reporter contacts me I'm not shy about sharing how I think about something that interests both of us.

Just remember to bite your tongue if you have to, but stay civil even when you would like to fly off the handle. Recently, U.S. Senator Marco Rubio, R-FL, called for more civility in our society. He said, "I want people to think about our politics here in America, because I'm telling you guys I don't know of a civilization in the history of the world that's been able to solve its problems when half of the people in a country absolutely hate the other half of the people in that country." He was absolutely right. I am constantly amazed at how vile otherwise reasonable people can be when they are disappointed politically.

There is no quicker way to lose an argument than to let your anger dominate your discussion. Even if you are not as persuasive as you would like to be, try to stay calm, gather your facts and hope you get another shot at the person who disagrees with you. One of the worst outcomes of an argument is to feel like you won, but in the process you lose a good friend.

•   •   •

It is amazing how uncivil we are becoming as a nation. There is evidence throughout our society of a breakdown in our socializing skills. We seem to be losing our ability or our willingness to control our emotional outbursts.

Road rage has become a serious problem. According to Roadragers.com "others can be just as enraged as you are, and their reaction to you may be downright dangerous." Drivers.com says that road rage is more than driving aggressively. It involves criminal behavior.

In April 2007, a Colorado driver was convicted of first-degree murder for causing the deaths of two motorists. He will serve a mandatory sentence of two consecutive life terms. Clearly it's safer to never give in to road rage.

However, it's not just drivers who don't recognize societal limits on offensive behavior. Examples run throughout our society. It is frightening how often we see news reports of kids being beaten on school buses while drivers do nothing to stop it. Go to a movie theater and see how many people plop their dirty shoes on the headrest of the seat in front of them or carry on a loud conversation as though they were sitting in their living room, with no regard for the people around them.

Walk through a mall and listen to the profanity that teenagers use in casual conversations. And how many times have you seen someone sitting at the table next to you in a restaurant pull out a cell phone and start a conversation you don't care to listen to with your dinner?

The truth is we are becoming a more selfish and egocentric society, interested mostly in our own needs and wants, without caring much about other people. If we would occasionally think about the effect our conduct has on those around us, maybe some day we could regain the civility we once had as a nation.

One of the reasons I prefer to write is the ability to research my topics thoroughly before I set pen to paper, and the absence of malice in the publishing process. While I sometimes disagree with a friend when I write an article, I don't know of any time I have lost a friend because of something I've written. You can disagree without being disagreeable. Sometimes people lose their composure in face-to-face confrontations, yet they maintain their cool when they are writing. I find that writing really can satisfy the soul in ways that a face–to–face confrontation just cannot satisfy!

One of the things I especially like to write about every year is Christmas. The nature of our society is changing so dramatically that it may be unrecognizable to some of our older citizens. The changes are especially noticeable during the Christmas season.

In recent years there has been a serious effort to remove God from the marketplace. Fifty years ago, between 85-90 percent of Americans claimed to be Christian; now that figure is closer to 65-70 percent.

Fifty years ago, having a crèche on display in the town square during the Christmas season was common. Today, despite the fact that Christmas is a national holiday and the government shuts down to celebrate the holiday, local governments forbid the public display of a crèche on government property. For that matter, they forbid the public display of anything calling attention to the religious aspects of Christmas. Mention of Santa Claus is OK, but the actual celebration of the birth of Jesus Christ is not.

I can find no statistics that suggest non-Christians refuse to honor this holiday. They don't insist on working. They take the day off with pay, even as some of them debunk the occasion and ridicule our celebration of the birth of Jesus Christ.

Equally perplexing, local governments honor the national holiday, but often forbid public display of anything calling attention to the reason for the season. A government organization can pay its employees to take the day off to celebrate

Christmas and then forbid them from doing so where they work or on any public property. Does that make any sense?

In recent years, department store employees began to express "holiday" greetings instead of Christmas greetings, until a public uproar drove them to restore the "Merry Christmas" greeting.

Fifty years ago December Christmas programs were ubiquitous. There was no Christmas issue anywhere in the United States. Merchants and citizens proudly strung lights and wreaths on their property, hung Christmas banners, and decorated Christmas trees. Some businesses even set aside time during the workday to serve eggnog and celebrate their last workday before Christmas.

But our shifting attitudes about Christmas may be symptomatic of even greater changes in our communities. Some authorities believe the disintegration of the family is the single most destructive element changing our society. This Christmas, if you know of a fatherless child, think about how you might be able to brighten up the lives of the mother and her children.

Despite the changing nature of our Christmas celebrations, Christmas is still a joyous and festive season. *Peace on earth and goodwill towards men* is still the operative phrase during this period. So, whenever you get the chance, say "Merry Christmas" and do whatever you can to share the blessings of Christmas with others.

But most of all, whether or not you live in our wonderful part of Florida, remember that *Jesus is still the reason for the season.* If you let Him He will fill your heart with joy and give you respite from all the negatives things happening around the world. It's a time to honor his second commandment. *Love your neighbor.* Don't let the Grinch steal your Christmas.

Success

For too many people success is centered on money. Most people would probably consider a billionaire to be supremely successful. How much is a billion dollars? A billion dollars is one thousand million dollars, a staggering sum of money that most of us can't even imagine. We throw that term around constantly without really thinking about how much money it really is. And consider that there are multi-billionaires; President Donald J. Trump claims to be worth $10 billion, an unimaginable sum of money. If you want to really challenge your imagination, consider that Bill Gates is alleged to be worth $90 billion. Even more mind-boggling is the fact that according to Forbes there are 540 billionaires in the United States.

How long would it take you to save a billion dollars? Suppose you were born on the same day Jesus Christ was born, that you were still alive today and that you had been able to save money at the fantastic rate of one penny for every second you lived. At that rate it would take you more than a thousand years to save one billion dollars.

What could you do with a billion dollars? You could build 100 libraries at a cost of $10 million each; 20 high schools at a cost of $50 million each; hire 5,000 school teachers and pay them $40,000 per year for five years; or give 2,000 worthy students a $50,000 college scholarship. On the other hand, one billion dollars invested well could make a series of spectacular university endowments.

For some people being able to do all of those things would surely resonate as their sound of success. But for me, success isn't how much money I have. It isn't anything commercial. It isn't the sound of money or the sound of a powerful automobile engine, or my name on a billboard, or anything material you can think of.

Incidentally, I said in my preface that I would let you know at the end of this book what my sound of success is. *Success for me is the sound of my wife breathing when she is lying next to me in bed.* Getting her to marry me nearly 60 years ago was the most successful thing I've ever done. And as long as I have that sound next to me I'm a happy man. Nothing else I ever did with my life has given me the same pleasure and sense of success as having her as my wife for all these years. I suggest you think about the things that are really important to you when you decide what your sound of success really is.

Meanwhile I will continue to write. I'm confident Dr. Al Sullivan, the Boston University professor who had so much influence on how I write, would be proud of what I've done over the years. At least I hope so.

I am sure there are a lot of articles still buried in my mind, but I am not clairvoyant enough to know what they might be. I also imagine there is yet another book somewhere in my future, but as I bring this one to a close I have no idea what might interest me enough to write that book.

I can tell you that my wife hopes I don't write any more books. When I do, I become so single-focused that she doesn't see much of me away from my computer. But I never know what will be the inspiration for my next writing project.

Epilogue

Just in case it hasn't registered with you, I am a blessed man! I have a great God, a great wife and a great life. God has been ever present in my life. He has blessed me with a great family, many of whom have sadly already passed, great friends for whom I will be forever thankful, a strong and loving marriage, and a lifetime of exciting challenges manifested in a wonderful series of career opportunities.

Looking back over my life, I rarely thought God had blessed me with specific job opportunities, or with special loving friends. Like most people I just took for granted that I lived in a wonderful world and if I paid attention and applied my God given talents, I could overcome the poverty that represented my early years, and life would be good. But, I learned otherwise as I began to appreciate my blessings. That philosophy began with my mother who was the inspiration for much that was good in my early life.

My mother encouraged me at every step of the way as I followed my early inclination to pursue the example of my male family role models by entering the U.S. Navy. Later she encouraged me as I thought about pursuing an education beyond high school. Because of her inspiration, I was the first member of my family to go to college.

It also helped that she fell in love with Peggy early on in our courtship, and she thought our marriage was an excellent idea. Even today, 14 years after my mother's death, the memory of her example as she raised five children by herself, after my father abandoned us, is the strongest lesson of morality, integrity, courage, and self-sacrifice, I ever got as a young man. I will forever be grateful to my mother. Everything good about me came from her.

I will also always cherish the love my wife has given me. We struggled mightily during the first 15 years of our marriage, as is often the case in marriages. There are no perfect marriages, but we eventually connected in an awesome way once we put God into the center of our marriage. I know widows and widowers who have been blessed with a second love late in life, but I cannot envision that ever happening to me. I simply cannot imagine loving anyone else the way I love Peggy. She was and is the woman of my dreams! I cannot even conceive of life without her.

That became foremost in my mind in 2017 when she was diagnosed with ovarian cancer. Even now we are in the midst of six months of chemotherapy treatments, with surgical removal of her ovaries, and I am reminded every day that life is fragile at best and I must cherish every day with her.

Also I can't remember a time when I didn't think I was a Christian, with God and Jesus as the center of my belief system. You may not want to read about my faith, but it is central to my life and I feel compelled to mention it as I close out this memoir.

From my earliest years as an elementary student in a Roman Catholic school, and my years as an altar boy, I took it for granted that I was a Christian. However, over the years I drifted away from the church, even though I never drifted away from God. I always believed in the concept of sin, prayer, redemption, and the need for salvation.

In 2004 after Peggy and I tried out many Catholic and Protestant churches in Brevard County, Florida, we literally stumbled onto Calvary Chapel Melbourne (CCM), and fell in love with the Calvary Chapel experience, shepherded by Pastor Mark Balmer. CCM is a multi-site church (one church in many locations), sharing God's message through live streaming video at the Viera and Sebastian, Florida campuses. CCM teachings stream on the web, Roku and the radio.

There are many pastors serving the more than 10,000 people who attend CCM every week, but Pastor Balmer is the principal pastor who established CCM in 1992. He is a gifted speaker who gives weekly 60-minute teachings that rival the quality of those given by Pastor Billy Graham, Pastor David Jeremiah, or Pastor Chuck Smith, the well-known founder of Calvary Chapel Costa Mesa, California.

Calvary Chapel Melbourne brought me back to God in a way I had not experienced in many years. In 2004, my wife and I accompanied Pastor Balmer. and about 70 other people, on a tour of Israel, and in the middle of the Sea of Galilee I felt a special connection with God. I cannot explain it other than to say I felt His Presence while we were praying at sea. We returned to Israel and the Sea of Galilee in 2007 and, while I didn't experience quite the same emotion, I again knew I was in the midst of special experience that gave me a deepened spiritual awareness.

After we returned to Melbourne, Florida in 2004, I attended the main CCM campus in West Melbourne. Then I began ushering at Calvary Chapel Melbourne/Viera when it was established in 2007 and continue to this day. For me ushering is more than helping people find their seats, it is a way to greet them with a warm handshake or a hug that says: "Welcome! While you are here you are in a special place where God and his son Jesus is the central focus."

Each of the Calvary Chapel locations offers weekend services in a relaxed environment (casual dress) in which the focus is on God's Words and His salvation message. Each service includes 30 minutes of praise and worship music, followed by a 60-minute lesson taught by Pastor Balmer or another staff or guest pastor.

For those of you who can't imagine attending a Megachurch, we have small groups of 10-20 people who get together during the week to study the Word, pray for one another and bond in a more intimate setting. CCM is a bible focused and God inspired church that appealed to me from the first moment I stepped into its sanctuary.

Even as I worship at CCM, a nondenominational church, I cherish my years as a Roman Catholic. Protestants who think Catholics are not Christians mystify me, just as do Catholics who think Protestants are not Christian. Jesus Christ is the central focus of both. They have different rituals but the salvation message is the foundation of all Christian churches, with a singular focus on the Triune God. He loves us all! Catholics and Protestants who don't understand that are a mystery to me.

I would welcome comments from anyone who disagrees with this premise, just as I look forward to hearing from anyone who reads this memoir. Feel free to contact me at dgill000@aol.com. I've written five books during the last four years, four of them about America. Check out my web page at www.donaldgilleand.com. You will discover that I am in love with America! In my opinion it has no equal anywhere else in the world.

It doesn't matter whether you agree or disagree with anything I've written. The primary reason I write is to stimulate public discussion of topically sensitive issues. If you disagree with any of my opinions let me know. I'm sure I'll learn something from you.

Donald L. Gilleland

CPSIA information can be obtained
at www.ICGtesting.com
Printed in the USA
FFOW01n2311010318
45414135-46113FF